On the Shore
of the Sundown Sea

On the Shore

Design by John Beyer

of the Sundown Sea

T. H. WATKINS

Illustrated by Earl Thollander

351091

SIERRA CLUB   SAN FRANCISCO • NEW YORK   1973

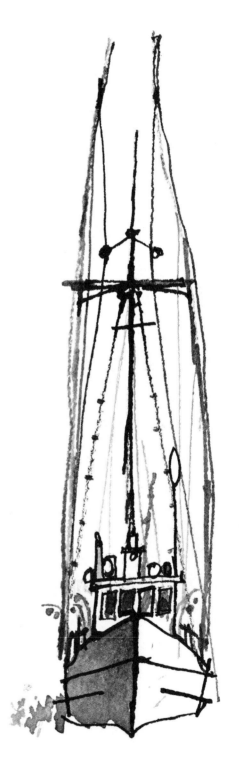

The Sierra Club, founded in 1892 by
John Muir, has devoted itself to the
study and protection of the nation's
scenic and ecological resources—
mountains, wetlands, woodlands, wild
shores, and rivers. All club publications
are part of the nonprofit effort the club
carries on as a public trust. There are
more than 40 chapters coast to coast, in
Canada, Hawaii, and Alaska. Participa-
tion is invited in the club's program to
enjoy and preserve wilderness every-
where. Address: 1050 Mills Tower, San
Francisco, California 94104.

This book is for Joan: My Love

Contents

Our noisy years seem moments in the being
Of the eternal Silence: truths that wake,
    To perish never:
Which neither listlessness, nor mad endeavor,
    Nor Man nor Boy,
Nor all that is at enmity with joy,
Can utterly abolish or destroy!

Hence in a season of calm weather
    Though inland far we be,
Our souls have sight of that immortal sea
    Which brought us hither,
    Can in a moment travel thither,
And see the children sport upon the shore,
And hear the mighty waters rolling evermore.

——WILLIAM WORDSWORTH

Prologue

ALL THE PEDDLERS of a lost, bittersweet nostalgia had been telling me for years that you can't go home again. I should have believed them, I suppose, but a stubborn little kernel of yearning would not let me. Besides, I was with someone I loved, and when you are stricken with that "first, fine, careless rapture," it seems profoundly important to explain yourself, unstitch the layers that cover secret dreams in an effort to blot out the fearful possibility that you are not much different from anyone else. And so I launched our vague pilgrimage, she willing and tolerant in her own affection, gently amused at my intensity, perhaps suspecting the truth I had chosen to ignore.

The homeland to which I was taking her had nothing to do with my home town, which had long since succumbed to progress, the landmarks which guide memory either destroyed or altered beyond recognition. No, this homeland was the most precious part of the geography of my youth, a stretch of Southern California coast that lay between Salt Creek Beach in the north and San Clemente in the south—little more than ten miles in length, but once a whole continent to a child's eye, a landscape which had given me my first and last taste of what freedom might be. And it was here, like a snake shedding winter skins, I had passed from one image of myself to another in the journey from boy to man.

We set out from Culver City southwest of Los Angeles,

where we had been covering the 1970 auction of MGM's forty-year collection of props and costumes (a genuine wake in the land of celluloid dreams; perhaps it should have told me something). Near Long Beach, we abandoned the freeway and took to Highway 1, the old coast highway, which was what I would have had to do in the age before freeways; if you're going to revisit your past, you might as well do it up right. Most of the trip was a dismal experience, as it always had been, for there are parts of Highway 1 in this region that are as ugly as any stretch of highway in the United States, an attentuated wilderness of neon, cheapjack used-car lots, dreary bars, drive-in restaurants made of weathered plastic, service stations greasy with age, "mission-style" motels with missing roof tiles and peeling plaster, and on the ocean side black pumps that dipped and rose, dipped and rose in long lines, busily sucking oil from beneath the sand. Over it all, as if a brush fire were raging somewhere out of sight, lay a reddish-gray pall of smog. Joan quickly developed a pained look between the eyes.

The smog thinned gradually as we traveled south past Seal Beach and Huntington Beach, catching occasional glimpses of surf between convalescent hospitals and oil pumps. By the time we reached Newport Beach, the smog had nearly disappeared. So had Newport Beach, as I remembered it. It was once an aging, quietly charming place that had been half-fishing village and half tourist-town, with a rickety old pier from which I had fished for mackerel more than once. Now I could hardly find it, what with a freeway interchange, motels, shopping centers, and what appeared to be a high-rise department store. The hills were alive with condominiums.

"Jesus," I muttered. "Where did all this come from?"

"How long has it been since you were here?"

I had to think. "Twenty-two, twenty-three years, maybe." In Southern California, that was more than enough time for a life-style to vanish. Two or three life-styles.

South of Newport Beach the highway began to hug the land much closer to the sea, rising with the coast as it alternately swelled to hills and bluffs, then sank, roller-coaster fashion, into hollows with crescent-shaped beaches. Much of the rolling grassland was crowded with spanking new housing developments that clustered like immobile lemmings at the very edge of the sea, but in the late morning sun the ocean flashed with the brassy sheen I remembered. If you looked at it too long, your eyes would begin to ache from the glare and the heat of it.

Laguna Beach had not changed appreciably. Even in my childhood it had been an artsy-craftsy place, and the tradition lingered—even flourished, to all appearances. It was still a town that took its manufactured Mediterranean heritage seriously, with much tropical vegetation punctuated by little white-washed houses with red tile roofs. There were parking meters now in the short downtown section through which the highway ran, strung with block-after-block of pottery shops, galleries, bookstores, leather emporiums, sliver-sized restaurants, and bungalow-like motels almost hidden by bougainvillea and palm trees. Two noticeable differences were the presence of long-haired young people, the men with hairy faces, the women in worn, artfully patched Levis, and the absence of the red-bearded old man who had once stood on the street corners in raggle-taggle clothing bellowing welcome to passing motorists as the town's unofficial greeter. I supposed he had died, his memory shoveled into the dustbin of yesterdays like the ramshackle fishing village of Newport. At least the town had not replaced him with a Disneylike, walking, talking replica—or even a hand-hewn granite statue along carefully modern lines, which would have been much more its style.

Next stop: Salt Creek Beach, about five miles south of Laguna. Here was the base of my memoried youth, for it was here that I had spent at least half of my summers by the sun-down sea. It had been a gentle little scoop out of the coast with a good line of surf, a beach littered here-and-there with clumps of dead kelp, and under its one rocky point, a collection of tidepools harboring a miniature submarine world. Just to the south of the curving beach a little dirt road had crawled between the bluffs and the sea, dotted with occasional outhouses and communal water faucets, and it had been along this stretch that most of our camps had been made.

When we reached the site of the beach, I pulled to the

shoulder of the road and stopped, glaring balefully at another outraged memory. The little terraced bluff overlooking the beach had once harbored a collection of summer tents; now it harbored a collection of summer homes for the rich folks. The little road that led down to the beach—asphalt now—was chained off. Private Road. No Trespassing. Gone was the two-bit general store near the highway. Gone was the withering kelp on the beach, which glistened now as if it had been laundered. Gone was anything I could fix my memory on, except the sea itself.

"Well, hell," I said. "It ain't fair."

"*Life* is not fair," she reminded me.

My expectations lay tattered, but I have always been a stubborn type. I pulled back to the road for yet another guidepost: Dana Point, a thrust of land that had been the most awesome Presence in this childhood landscape, an Olympus whose mute bulk I had had the temerity to challenge once and only once. They couldn't have destroyed Dana Point, I reasoned—it was just too damned big.

They hadn't. As we topped the slope above Salt Creek Beach, the point came into view about two miles south of us, probing into the sea like an inquisitive finger. In some lights and times of day, I knew, it would at this distance appear gray-blue against the darker ocean, as vague and transient to the eye as the wisps of a dream. This day, in this light, it was etched clearly, crowned by a tonsure of iceplant and sea grass; below that, it tumbled toward the sea in a great rush of tan-and-white sandstone. At the foot of the plunging cliff, a single great block of stone stood isolated, collared by breaking waves—testament to where the point had once ended, in some dim epoch.

The point was not as large as I remembered it, but I had expected that. The giants of youth lose stature in middleage. At a height less than 150 feet above the sea, this little mass of land was no match for the looming, primordial slopes of the Big Sur Coast, or parts of the North Coast. Still, it was the largest chunk of anything along this stretch of the South Coast, quite respectable even when robbed of the dimensions of memory. And I knew something now that I had not known in my youth: Dana Point was one of California's earliest and most enduring literary landmarks, for it was on its rim that Richard Henry Dana had stood in the spring of 1834 and tossed dried cowhides to the beach below. Stripped from the backs of tough black Mexican cattle, the hides were as stiff and heavy as sheets of plywood, yet they fluttered and swooped and tumbled in the wind like the autumn leaves of Dana's native New England (where the hides were destined to be made into shoes and boots for the Great Unwashed). On the beach, men retrieved the hides from the sand, put them on their heads, and waded through the surf to waiting longboats, which delivered great stacks of them to the brig *Pilgrim*, bobbing a hundred yards offshore in the uncertain anchorage of Dana Cove. In a brief and eloquent passage, the whole scene had been limned by Dana in *Two Years Before the Mast*, one of the greatest books ever written about the sea.

A few minutes after sighting the point, we pulled into the little parking lot on its top, placed there for the convenience of tourists who wished to gaze out from what had since become a State Historic Landmark. To their further convenience, a little wooden observation tower, complete with ten-cent telescopes, had been erected on the curving rim of the cliff above the cove, perhaps very near to where Dana himself had once stood. I took Joan's hand as we stepped into the observation tower and walked toward its farthest railing; what the hell—a man isn't privileged to present a moment of high drama every day.

The drama was high enough, but someone had been mucking about with the screenplay. There was no cove of curling surf, white sand, and rocks below us. What there was below us was a huge marina under construction. Where the sand and surf had once danced their primeval saraband, a broad expanse of well-packed earth spread over the beach, covering rocks, water, and sand alike with engineered fill. From this massive foundation, large finger piers extended a hundred yards or so out into the water. There was nothing makeshift or impermanent about them; they appeared to be made of concrete, probably poured right down to the floor of the cove. Farther out, beyond the fill and the piers, a long rock-fill breakwater was tacked on to the tip of the point.

Behind this breakwater the cove was as still and peaceful as a pond in a meadow. On the big fill itself, scabrous yellow earth-moving equipment—bulldozers, graders, and the like—scuttled over the ground like beetles, their gutteral grunts and roars washing up the slope of the cliff and obliterating the sound of wind and water.

I expressed myself in one four-letter word as eloquent as it was inadequate. Joan took my arm without saying anything. We did not yet know each other too well, but she knew that time had pierced me. I knew her well enough to know that she was saying she understood, but of course she did not. How could she? I was not sure myself why I felt suddenly hollow, stripped of certitudes. I suppose it may have been that all those things in which I had expressed belief for a long period of time had finally touched me personally and made me feel, as well as know, what I believed. Imagine a man believing in miracles all his life and finally being privileged to witness one; or a man knowing that death could be ugly, then watching his best friend ripped up the middle by a land mine in a moist Vietnam jungle.

For years, I had written about man and his assault on the land, about the threat to the fragility of life—all life. I had written about the cutover stands of redwood trees, dead and dying fish, deserts guttered by motorcycles and fourwheel drive vehicles, overdeveloped coastal regions, dammed rivers, poisoned bays, disappearing wilderness areas, mismanaged national forests, overcrowded national parks, potential urban parks bargained away to the speculator's itch. First-rate polemic, all of it, I liked to think, well-reasoned, to the point, and written out of conviction.

Yet much of it was done in the style a good reporter brings to his work: just enough involvement to make the writing interesting, the rest a matter of figures, interviews, balanced speculations, and information organized to a logical conclusion. Nothing had raked across my personal nerve ends enough to abandon the detachment necessary to a good job of work. My mind had been geared to the inarguable intellectual precept that time was running out for man and the land he called home. But my heart had not found a home for anger, or even understanding. Now it had, for I had been robbed—me, personally—of my memories. Those blind and possibly uncontrollable forces against which I had pitted my skills with such detached energy had *gotten* me.

When a man says he was stricken with the inspiration for a book in a single moment, or out of a single experience, he is probably lying; books are neither conceived nor made that easily. Yet I think I knew, standing on the rim above concretized Dana Cove, that someday, somehow there would have to be a book. Not a book of polemics or lamentations, but a book that honored what the coast had given me when it was the homeland of my youth, and what those parts of it that remained still gave to me.

But the book was tomorrow. I still had today to deal with. We returned to the car and sped off down the Coast Highway, past Doheny Beach State Park, past Capistrano Beach, and on into San Clemente, which as a kind of mild antidote to Dana Point had neither disappeared nor been entirely remodeled. With the exception of two or three additional motels, a little more neon, a shopping center, and the San Diego Freeway, which sliced through the eastern fringe of the town, San Clemente had not succumbed to the fever of growth as near as I could tell. The same four-story hotel was still the tallest building in town; the same theatre still advertised the same kind of fifth-run movie; the same hamburger stand, I was sure, still served the same cardboard hamburgers and chalky malts (with an inflated price, of course). Not even the vague presence of the President in his western White House had apparently been enough to shake the town out of its seaside torpor.

Between the southern edge of the town and San Clemente Beach State Park, a few miles down the road, the freeway was the dominant presence. The state park was the last card in my inadequate deck, and as we turned off the freeway onto the little road that led down a deep gully to the beach, I was relieved to see that it was not even as crowded as it sometimes had been in my youth. Nor had it changed appreciably. The parking area was still gravelled dirt, the little rest rooms still reeked of stale urine and a generation of wet bathing suits, and you still had to tiptoe gingerly across the tracks of the Santa Fe Railroad to make your way down to the beach, which edged some of the finest swimming surf in the world.

I turned to the waves, then, my first love, and waded through the troughs and the boiling surf of dying combers. Then I reached the cresting point, and reaching back into the experience of childhood, like a man jumping onto a bicycle after an absence of twenty years, I timed a large curling wave and dove under it, hearing the tumbling roar of its breaking just as I sliced into its fat base.

Coming up from that first wave was like a rebirth, a tiny triumph in a day of defeats. The joy and the release were not gone, nor was the challenge of knowing I was dealing with an element that could kill me. These were waves to be reckoned with—five, six, as much as eight feet from base to crest, with the power to stun the senses with awe, and sometimes honest terror. Yet, with the calculated abandon, if not the stamina, of my boyhood, I let the surf batter me mindless for God only knows how long, straining, diving, letting the waves carry my arched body like a pudgy surfboard, returning to do it again, miscalculating and being slammed into the sand with the force of a Mack truck. When I finally stepped out of the surf, spent, the sun had dipped several degrees and the northward-moving currents, which I had forgotten, had carried me more than a half a mile from where I had started. One shoulder was scraped raw by sand, and I could feel the sun stinging my back as I trudged down the beach. I knew I would be sore and miserable all night, and cursed myself for a middle-aged idiot. But for all my exhaustion and pain, my walk back to where Joan sat, one hand shading her eyes in search of me, was a parade of celebration. For a while, for a brief while, I had been privileged to experience again the outlines of my life. For an hour or so, I had indeed been home.

PART ONE
Freedom's Landscape

And I have loved thee, Ocean! and my joy
Of youthful sports was on thy breast to be
Borne, like thy bubbles, onward: from a boy
I wantoned with thy breakers. . . .
And trusted to thy billows far and near,
And laid my hand upon thy mane—as I do here.

——GEORGE GORDON, LORD BYRON

The Longest Hour

MY MOTHER has always been a woman of formidable convictions, and one of the most powerful of those convictions in my youth was that the ocean could kill the hell out of you. I can remember a litany of warnings against riptides, undertows, sting-rays, and especially cramps, a phenomenon I never once felt or witnessed, but which huddled in the shadows of my boyhood mind like the grisly spectre of Death itself. Cramps, it seemed, could sneak up on you at any time (preferably, however, when you were in water over your head) clutching at your vitals, forcing your knees to draw up, embryo-like, to your chin, leaving you helpless and, ultimately, drowned. It was a terrible thing to think about; therefore, I never thought about it.

My mother did think about it. She thought about it quite a lot, and had developed the theory that the only way to prevent the phenomenon was to wait a full hour after eating before going into the water. She enforced this rule with the implacable righteousness of an Old Testament prophet. No amount of piteous entreaty, logical argument, or simple pestering could move her. I waited, and to this day I do not believe she understands the exquisite torture it was. It was my first lesson in the truth of the relativity of time.

The first fifteen minutes or so could be whiled away by dabbling in the sand, perfecting techniques of sandcastle architecture or scribbling my name in ten-foot letters, announcing my presence to passing airplanes or seagulls. But that soon paled, and there was nothing left but to sit on the sand, waiting, sweating, feeling the sun bake my bones, watching it glint through the thin blade of a wave near the point of collapse, making it briefly as translucent as a sheet of stained glass, watching the netlike tracery of spent surf on the beach, watching it bubble and fade away, leaving the sand as smooth and polished as dark marble. And of course I listened, listened to the primeval rhythm of the waves, the *smack!* and roar of their breaking, their muted grumbling as they disintegrated in a rush toward shore, and the extended hiss of their dying on the sand. It was a song I knew as well as if I had written its chords myself, a Lorelei song that pulled at something so deep in me that it was past imagining or understanding.

For I think sometimes that I was born to hear that song in that time and place, and respond to its call. I have heard of some people who claim they can remember themselves all the way back to the floating, amniotic warmth of their beginnings. I cannot; at the same time, I cannot remember a time when I could not swim, when water was not a natural element for me, and perhaps one strand of unrealized memory did lead me back to that original dark. My mother tells a story: One summer, when I was just shy of three years old, she took me with my aunt and uncle to our local public swimming pool. Coming out of the dressing room with me in tow, she stopped to talk with someone. I escaped, and she did not notice my departure until she saw me scrambling up the ladder to the ten-foot diving board at the deep end of the pool. I remember none of this, but I can see it: I can see my mother shouting to my uncle on the other side of the pool; I can see him leaping to his feet and racing toward the edge of the pool as my chubby little body waddles full speed toward the end of the board; I can see myself launched over the water while my uncle dives frantically for the spot where I must enter; I can see our bodies strike almost simultaneously, his with a great spash, mine with a tiny plop; I can see him reaching out for me as I bob to the surface, clutching me in his arms while I laugh with a joy so absolute I am sure nothing I have felt since has equalled it.

I had experienced a kind of homecoming, I think, and for all the years of my childhood, that sense of returning to what was naturally mine never diminished. And so I sat on the sand under my mother's stern edict, not as a child deprived of play, but as a creature deprived of his element.

But then the wait ended, as even the worst of things usually do. At one point I would look back to my mother and she would nod. Filled with the elixir of release, I would bound straight toward those waves, her voice trailing after me, unheeded—"Don't go out too far!" I always entered the water with straightforward abandon, running knee-deep toward the first foaming mound of a dying wave, throwing myself into it with a sideways leap as it tumbled over my head and shoulders, giving me the first chill impact of water meeting sun-warmed skin. Free of its rolling thunder, I swam across the pool of its wake toward the next crumbling wave, ducking under it at precisely the right moment, feeling it tug and ruffle my legs in its passing. Then on to the next, and the next, until the waves rose slatelike and curving toward the sky. Home again.

And so began each of my summer days by the sundown sea. There were rarely more than thirty or forty such days each summer, yet between the ages of about nine and sixteen they were the distillation of each year, the best and brightest part, the part to be remembered during Southern California's winter rains and fogs, the part to be anticipated increasingly during the steadily-climbing temperatures of spring. They were days of learning; learning of myself, certainly, though I could not know it at the time, but mostly of the sea which welcomed me each June.

It was such a simple world, that landscape of summer. Its rules were laid down by sea and sun and wind, and there was little in them too complex for an eager young mind. Needing to know little, I knew all there was to know—the feel of moving surf, the frantic wriggling of sand beetles as they scrabbled into the wet sand in the wake of a wave, the crawling, variegated life of a tide pool, the hidden darkness of sea- and wind-carved caves, the moist weight of morning at low tide, the acrid iodine smell of kelp, the pressure of depth against my ears as I probed the miniature canyons of a smoky green underwater world.

First and always were the constant movements of the sea's ageless contest with the land, something to be studied with the concentration a Natty Bumppo might have given to the spoor of the forest—not out of fear, but out of a decent respect for the arts of survival. The currents that rippled between and through the waves could be antic and powerful at all times, but never more than during the pounding, wind-driven surf of late afternoon, when they frequently became small waves themselves, racing fiercely at right angles to the incoming waves and occasionally flowing straight back toward them, wave meeting wave with a tremendous clap and plume of spray. Such encounters were the most dramatic example of what my mother called "rip tides," and to be caught in the middle of one was like being trapped in the center of an explosion. It was not an experience that could kill, I suppose, (although my mother might argue otherwise), but it definitely was one to be avoided.

These cross and contrary currents were at least visible; others were more insidious. For several years my mother's cautions in regard to undertow were purely abstract. Having neither seen nor experienced one, I could not quite believe in it. Then, like Saul thrown from his horse, I acquired faith. During one afternoon of wave-chasing, I let the usual surge pull me toward a cresting wave, as usual—except that this time I was not pulled to the wave, I was pulled under it, and under the next, caught in the grip of a current so deep that my shoulders scraped against the sand of the bottom. Remembering my mother's admonitions never to struggle against it, I stifled the panic that rose in my throat like a fist and held my breath. How long I was under I have no idea, but it was probably no more than ten or fifteeen seconds before the undertow released me and I bobbed to the surface with a great whoosh of expelled breath. I was perhaps fifty yards beyond the breakers, and by the time I had paddled back to the waves and into shore, the trembling had ceased. I never did tell my mother of the experience. I was very young, but I was not stupid.

But staying out of the way of such things as rip tides and

undertow was largely a matter of learning to distrust mother ocean just enough. Having acquired that lingering distrust, I was free to dabble in the lexicon of the waves. They needed to be learned, those waves, for no two of them ever seemed to be alike in proportion or performance, and I had to know them in order to become part of them in their tumbling rush to the shore.

In later years I once toyed with the notion of becoming a surfboard rider. Borrowing a friend's board, I would paddle out beyond the breaker-line and kneel on it like the other surfers (a strangely quiet and isolated bunch when in the water), who floated under the sun like a collection of water-beetles, waiting for the ninth and perfect wave. When it, or a reasonable facsimile thereof, began swelling to a peak, we would all start racing with it, attempting to catch it on the breast beneath the trembling lip of its top, then standing and guiding the board in a slicing run down the slope of the wave, trying to stay ahead of the curling break, the board skittering and hissing through the water until the wave shriveled into surf. Sometimes I made it all the way; more often, I was caught in the break and wiped out, forced to dive deeply to avoid the tossing, suddenly lethal board —vehicle become weapon.

There was exhilaration enough in such rides, but I never learned to enjoy them as I enjoyed body surfing, which required its own skills and, I would insist, quite as much courage. Besides, when straddling a board and steering it through the water I was no more a part of the sea than a helmsman at the wheel of a freighter. I was using it, not joining it. Therein lay the difference that mattered to me, for like Byron's Childe Harold my joy was on the sea's breast to be borne, like her bubbles, onward (although I was then innocent of poetic allusions).

Proper body surfing demanded judgment, timing, and instinct in about equal proportions. There were no ninth waves that I can remember (who had time to count?), but there were waves to be avoided and waves to be embraced. To be avoided were the towering, curling monsters that rose at the far edge of the breaker line. These were not for riding, for they would simply bury you under a mountain of water, pounding and tumbling your helpless body like so much kelp. The shorter, thicker waves were better, and the best of all were the rare double- and triple-crested waves that would break two or three times on their way toward shore.

Having looked upon a wave and found it good, the next problem was to choose the right moment to begin swimming with it. Too late, and I would miss the break altogether, the wave skimming past and leaving me abandoned in its trough. Too soon, and I would find myself at the wave's foot as it broke, where I would be flipped and tossed without dignity. Precisely timed, my strokes would place me near the center of the wave as it began to break—and there was no mistaking the rightness of that moment. My body arched until it ached, and my arms straight at my sides, head and shoulders protruding like the figurehead on some China-bound clipper, I could feel the wave collapse under my chest, pulling me, enfolding me, accepting me, making me one with the timeless ritual of its breathtaking race for death on the sand. When conditions were perfect—rarely, but often enough—the thrust of a wave would carry me fifty or sixty yards until the beach brushed against my chest and stopped me. There I would lay for a brief time, spent like the wave that whispered its life out on the sand beyond me; spent, and filled with the inarticulated certainty that for a time I had become something more than what I was, something as mutely wondrous as the sea itself.

Time slipped by like oil on those summer mornings, but sooner or later I would hear my mother's voice competing with the waves, calling me in for lunch. Some interior clock almost always told me when this was about to happen, and at the right moment I would cast a shrewd eye shoreward to see her rise from her blanket and begin walking down to the beach. I would then keep my back toward her so that I might pretend for a while that I did not see or hear her. Some other instinct informed me when I had stretched the pretending to the point when she would be ready to have my father come in the water after me. Then I would turn and wave in surprise, seek out one more suitable wave, and come tumbling into shore. If she ever caught on to this one-sided game, she never let me know it.

There would be sandwiches then, inevitably gritty with sand but no less satisfying for it, and after them, once again, the interminable, damnable waiting. It was somewhat easier to endure in the afternoons, I have to admit. There was a certain sybaritic pleasure to be found in lying flat on my full belly in the warm sand while my mother gently kneaded suntan lotion into my back and legs. This lotion was one of her inventions, a home-made mixture of Johnson's baby oil and iodine in proportions she kept to herself. I have no idea whether the rather foul-smelling concoction's virtues had any basis in scientific fact. I do know that while it felt a little like being deep-fat fried, I cannot remember a time in my boyhood when I turned anything but a comfortable mahogany in a matter of days. It was only in later years, when I turned to commercial products for protection, that I experienced the incomparable agonies of sunburn.

But even the pleasures of sun and sand would begin to jade before the hour was gone. The sand would stick irritatingly to my well-oiled body, the sun become oppressive and sweat-making. The last minutes of this second-longest hour would be spent in petulant squirming until the blessing of my mother's nod sent me streaking back to the waves.

Usually in these afternoon sessions my father, and sometimes my mother, would join me. I preferred my father, for my otherwise ebullient and sometimes downright adventurous mother, the former ballet student and dance instructor who had eloped to Yuma, Arizona, with my father at the advanced age of seventeen, found little joy in the roisterous and unpredictable surf. Her pleasure was taken in the serene, gently-moving swells of the water beyond the breaker line, where she contentedly tread water for half an hour or forty-five minutes while my father and I bobbed around with her. There was some satisfaction for me in the fact that these were the only times I was normally allowed to swim beyond the breakers.

Normally my father was a man little given to exuberance. He lived very much within himself, spending the coin of his emotions frugally (although, since he ultimately fathered six children, he must have been susceptible to moments of genuine extravagance). My most enduring memory of him during my childhood was his quiet—not necessarily a taciturn or moody quiet, but one with an almost meditative quality, like a mathematics professor constantly chewing over some problem in advanced calculus. Yet hidden within his hoard of emotions was a profound and contrary sense of humor that released itself in laughter like water from a broken dam, full-throated and uproarious, laughter spent as unreservedly as Gene Fowler once said money should be spent, like "something to be thrown off the back end of trains." Early on, I developed for him a bag of fond tricks and a sense of the sardonic, all of it designed to prod loose that burst of laughter.

In the waves, my father laughed, laughed like a child out of prison. Supremely unathletic out of the water, *in* the water he performed with the finesse of an Olympian; the waves were his cross-bars and hurdles, and he knew them the way a track man knows the obstacles that test his skill and endurance. I suppose I learned as much about surfing from watching my father perform as I did from my own experience. It was a silent education in the logistics of waves, but more: it was a sharing, an unspoken communication that obliterated, for a time, the differences between us. I never felt closer to my father than when we were two arm-lengths apart, sliding side-by-side down the slope of a breaking wave, being plummeted shoreward and spewed out on the sand like a pair of otters, where we would stand, laughing, and loving each other in that laughter.

Such moments never seemed to last long enough, for with all the visible joy my father took in the sea, the poor man was as thin-blooded as a bird, and bitterly vulnerable to cold. Sooner or later, his lips would begin to tremble . Stubbornly, he would resist as long as he could, but when his teeth began to chatter he would give it up, his long, heavy-shouldered body blue with cold as he stepped from a final wave and strode across the sand, back to the warmth of the sun and the deeps of his unexplained meditations.

I would be alone again, but that had rarely bothered me,

36

in or out of the sea. As the oldest, by four years, of six children, I had quickly learned the solace of what E. B. White once called the "gift of privacy, the jewel of loneliness." For another two or three hours I would remain in the water, until the sea revoked its welcome, as it always did, with the ebb tide of late afternoon. The waves became short, thick, and punishing, digging my body into the sand more and more often, filling my ears and mouth with grit. The cross-currents became more fierce, the undertow harder to withstand. Since morning, I had been privileged to feel the pulse of all time and life, but this was the hour for the sea to assert the essential savagery of its contest with the land. It was no place for a boy, or even a man.

The end of each of these long summer days was a waltz of sunny pleasure, of more sand castles, of explorations, of pebble and seashell hunts, of mindless, exhilarated running whose only purpose was movement. As the sun curved out of sight, I would change to sweat shirt and jeans, after which there would be dinner, served hot from a campstove on a paper plate and wolfed with the undiscriminating hunger of childhood. As twilight slipped into darkness, there would usually be a pit fire in the sand with flames to feed and watch while my mother bedded down the last, whimpering, heavy-lidded member of her younger brood. I was allowed to choose my own bed-time, but I rarely lasted until the flames had become embers.

I would crawl into my sleeping bag on the sand (another privilege; my brothers and sisters were tent-bound) in the muted, flickering glow of the dying fire. Behind me I would hear the soft, indistinct voices of my mother and father as they nursed a final beer before retiring to their own double-width bag beyond the firelight, and ahead of me the phosphorescent sea muttering to the night. Wrapped in the cocoon of my body's warmth, I would hug the certainty of tomorrow like a chalice, staring up at the awesome scatter of stars and wondering hugely about the beginnings and the ends of things.

The Planned Environment

T HERE IS AN INSTINCT loose in the family of man to do-
mesticate the wilderness. We are long past the age
when we could pile our wordly goods in a wagon,
throw an axe over our shoulder, and with a few other like-
minded people crawl into the wilds, pick a likely spot, kill a
few Indians, clear fields, lay out a township, build homes
and stores, and begin selling lots to one another. Yet the instinct remains, dormant during the winter months, blossom-
ing with virulence each spring and summer in any one of
hundreds of state and national parks across the land. In
America, at least, we are a race of frustrated pioneer settlers.
"Camping out," I sometimes think, is less a matter of rec-
reation than of cultural identity.

On its simplest level, the instinct is reflected by nothing
more complicated than a tent erected on a tiny plot of ground
surrounded by scores of similar tents. It offers shelter,
warmth, and a degree of privacy, and that is about all. Yet,
depending on the affluence and determination of the individual, the instinct can reach startling heights of sophistica-
tion. One of the most astonishing things I have ever seen
was the setup of a modern family of four in a small state park
on the Northern Coast. Their Conestoga wagon was a thirty-
foot motor home whose umbilical cords had been plugged
into available water and electricity. Along its side a little

cabana had been erected, complete with folding tables and aluminum patio furniture. Two relatively quiet Yamaha trailbikes provided local transportation. During the afternoon, a stereo set played a pleasant selection of soft rock or Mantovani records, depending upon whether the teenagers were present. In the late afternoon, the father would barbecue hamburgers on a portable grill, and as evening fell, the family would gather around the television set, its flickering, blue-white glow lighting their passive, contented faces. Here was *home*, beGod; let not bears and tigers intrude.

Bereft of such stunning luxuries, my mother and father did the best they could on the beaches of Southern California twenty-five years ago. Under the quietly imaginative direction of my father, their best was quite good, making up in ingenuity what it lacked in affluence. A reluctant, if competent, handyman at home, he became happily camp-wise on the beach; one of the most permanent memories I have is the image of him standing in the sand with the coil of rope in one hand and a hatchet in the other, his eyes glazed with thought behind his glasses as he considered how and where he might fix things up just a little bit better. He usually figured it out.

One of the first considerations he had to face was the simple matter of transporting himself, my mother, five—and later, six—children, one dog, camping gear, clothing, and a three-week supply of food the seventy miles between the little town of Colton and the coast. Even if such things as thirty-foot motorized homes had been available in those years they would have been ridiculously beyond our means, and the ultimate solution was a 1939 eight-passenger Buick, a blue-gray behemoth of a machine which my father purchased shortly after the war. It was the closest thing to a new car he had ever owned, and he was inordinately proud of it. Its purchase, however, had been a matter of no small consequence.

In our tiny, thin-walled frame house in Colton, my two brothers and I tucked into one bedroom, my two sisters in another, my mother and father in a third, there were no secret conversations, and for days I eavesdropped on high level kitchen discussions between my mother and father on the subject of the "new" car. The problem, I gathered, was one of juggling figures which almost always came out short, in spite of the inescapable fact that the family had simply outstripped the capacity of the old black sedan we had owned for some five years. Besides, even in an age in which the phrase "planned obsolescence" had not yet entered the language, the sedan was more than ten years old and fading fast. My father would mutter, scratching pencil on paper, adding, subtracting, dividing, and multiplying out loud, and always seemed to come out with the same answer: "There's no way we can do it."

"We have to do it," my mother would reply with a purely romantic disregard for the facts of the matter. "We'll just have to rob Peter to pay Paul." It was her battle cry.

Somehow, Peter was indeed robbed to pay Paul, and one afternoon my father came steaming home in the Buick. With the exception of highway trucks or the locomotives down at the Southern Pacific Railroad Station on the edge of town, I suppose that Buick was the largest moving thing I had ever seen. It was an impressive beast, looming like a dreadnought above me in the bulbous contours typical of Buicks of that vintage. As the family gathered around the beast, my mother, who had not seen it before, wore a stunned look on her face. "Well," she said slowly," well, it's a big one, all right."

With totally uncharacteristic volubility, my father ticked off the car's features like a barker touting the wonders of the fat lady at a circus. He showed us the spare tire snuggled under its cover in the wheel-well of the right front fender, and demonstrated the ease of its removal. He opened up the capacious trunk that sat like a bustle on the rear of the car. He spread wide the two rear doors and showed us the little folding chairs that were attached to the back of the front seat, pointing out that these, with the regular back seat, provided enough room for all five of us kids, leaving the front seat for him and my mother alone, a privilege they had not enjoyed for some time. He lifted the great blue snout of the car's hood, exposing an engine that looked big enough to power a tank, talking glibly about the manifold virtues of the "straight-8," although I am sure he was quite as ignorant of such things then as I am today. In response to much jumping up and down and importunate squealing, he bundled us all into the car for the maiden run.

The Buick drove heavily and quietly, with only two or three inconsequential rattles; the engine performed with a muted, steady, deep-throated hum, and just the barest click of tappets; the tires hissed over the surface of the road. It was the epitome of power, weight, and class—a *substantial* machine. After about fifteen minutes, my father zipped it around the corner and came to a liquid stop in front of the house, snapping off the ignition with a little flourish. "My God, honey," my mother said. "This isn't a car—it's a yacht."

My father laughed uproariously, and from that moment forward the Buick was nicknamed the Yacht.

The Yacht was our Rosinante for the next several years, faithfully lumbering between Colton and the coast repeatedly from spring to fall, burning up prodigious amounts of gasoline but failing us only rarely. Like Don Quixote's rickety steed, I suppose, the Yacht was in reality "lean, bony, and unsound," memory investing it with virtues it did not possess and exaggerating those that it did. Yet I remember it with an affection that has not been granted to any one of the ungodly number of automobiles with which I have been connected since. How could it be otherwise? The Yacht was my link between home and homeland.

Preparations for home-making in the wilderness, such as it was, began days before our annual vacation. First it was necessary to haul the tent out from the garage, where it had reposed since the previous summer, so that it could be aired for a while. This was no minor task. My father had bought it at an Army-Navy surplus store (back in the days when surplus *was* surplus), and it seemed large enough to have served as a headquarters tent; perhaps it had. Some fifteen feet long by ten wide and seven high, it was an olive drab in color and of a material that had the general weight and consistency of chain mail. Getting it erected in our back yard was like hoisting a dead man over a clothesline. Once up, it hung in evil-looking folds until its own weight pressed it

42

out. The airing was necessary mainly because some antebellum form of chemical had been added to the fabric as a water repellent, and the thing always steamed with a spectral stink for days. This, combined with the fact that it trapped heat, made the tent about as habitable as a Mississippi chickenfat factory. In addition, one of the principle frustrations of my father's life was the matter of disappearing tent stakes. Every summer, no matter how carefully he had packed them away the year before, he always seemed to come up short on his tent stakes. Muttering grimly, he would spend hours scrabbling around in the garage for three or four missing tent stakes. He almost never found them.

While my father hunted for tent stakes (and bought new ones), resurrected and cleaned the camp stove and Coleman lanterns, repaired tarpaulins ripped by last year's winds, and had the Yacht looked over by the local mechanic, my mother went through her own summer ritual. Much of this had to do with laying in supplies, a matter of considerable importance to a family with five children, any one of whom was frequently hungry enough to eat the paint off a house. Bulk was of primary interest under the circumstances, and the menu was inclined to be plain, basic, and containerized: canned tuna, canned salmon, Spam (the definitive proletarian food), canned corn, canned peas, canned kidney beans for chile, canned pork and beans, and canned fruits (we were much beloved by S & W Foods and the Campbell's people). Some variety was provided by hamburger patties, pork chops, and, in relatively flush times, slabs of round steak, all of these precooked and packed with lard in mason jars for preservation, since the closest thing to a refrigerator we had was a small portable ice chest whose primary function was to chill my father's beer and his children's milk. Breakfasts normally consisted of sundry dry cereals that either snapped, crackled, popped, or simply lay quietly in the bowl sopping up milk and sugar; we all loved it. Peanut butter and my mother's own hand-canned preserves and jellies were the staples of our summer lunches.

For as long as two weeks such preparations would go on, a maddening stretch of time. Unlike my brothers and sisters, I was old enough to be riven by the anxieties of expectation, yet too young to gain any solace from the preparations themselves. I was a nervous spectator to my father's pre-camp chores and my mother's list-making and grocery-buying, and my nights were fevers of anticipation. Yet the earth would always turn the required number of times and the morning of departure always arrive. The night before, my father would have washed the Yacht and attached a small open trailer borrowed from a friend, into which he scientifically packed a genuine mattress for him and my mother (incipient sybarites, both of them), the tent and tarpaulins, the camp stove and lanterns, army cots, pillows, sleeping bags, borrowed card tables, extra bedding, canvas chairs, rope, shovel, hatchet (the tools of his avocation), food, pots, pans, utensils, dishware, clothing, dog food, and whatever books my mother happened to be reading at the time. Crammed to the scuppers, the trailer would then be covered by a final tarpaulin, laced down as tight as a drumskin.

My father was addicted to early risings on vacation mornings, but no more than me. Like a programmed computer, my eyes popped open at the first flush of dawn, and I would lie in bed listening to the whispered breathing of my two brothers and waiting for the sound of my father's alarm clock. Its high-pitched buzzing, followed by the heavy thump of his bare feet on the floor at the side of the bed (I have said the walls were thin), was the signal to wake my brothers and sisters and help them get dressed. I was aided in this task by Buttons, the dog in my life, a beautifully marked dalmatian who crawled out from beneath my covers, shook herself, and began applying strategic face-licks to any child optimistic enough to think he could ignore the morning. Frequently, my father would have to fix breakfast, for my mother, bleary-eyed and sluggish, was only barely functional until well after her first cup of coffee. "I am not" she would report glumly, "a morning person."

Finally, dressed, fed, and bathroomed, we children all piled into the back of the Yacht, the three youngest on the large seat, the two oldest on the folding seats, and the dog on the floor between, usually with a leftover box of food or clothing. Then my father would do a quick run-through of the house, turning off lights, closing windows, checking the stove, and locking up, after which he would slip into the driver's seat, turn on the ignition, and start the car. While it idled, he would give my mother a long, meaningful look. "The can opener" (or the baby's diaper pins or her homemade suntan oil or her favorite spatula), was her almost inevitable statement. My father would laugh and retreat to the house to track down this last vagrant piece of equipment in the ritual of getting out of town.

I suppose I am belaboring the obvious when I say that there was a time in Southern California when automobile travel was not only a pleasure but an adventure. It was, quite simply, an age before automobiles became airconditioned capsules sucked along concrete arteries like brass bottles in the pneumatic messenger tubes of an old-time newspaper office. It is now possible, I understand, to get from Colton to the ocean in about forty-five minutes on the freeway, but how can anything be an adventure if it only takes forty-five minutes to get to it?

In my youth, it was an adventure. In the first place, my father was not a fast driver; moderate but sure was his unstated motto, and we rumbled along at speeds that rarely exceeded fifty miles an hour (in all honesty, I must admit that the Yacht may not have been *capable* of much more than fifty miles an hour, particularly with a full load). In the second place, even the relatively high-speed highways of that time were of a design that accepted and adapted to the contours and peculiarities of the land, instead of thrusting arrogantly through it or rising in disdain above it. Over the muffled rumble of the Yacht, the hiss of air past open windows, and the rythmic *whoosh* of passing telephone poles, you could hear the ghostlike trill of a meadowlark's song in an open field, or the repertoire of a mockingbird, or the high-pitched buzzing of cicadas. You could see hawks rising like leaves on the currents of the air, or buzzards circling with grisly patience over the unseen remains of some dead or dying loser in the lottery of existence, or redwing blackbirds fluttering insanely across the road in front of rushing automobiles, always seeming to time their flight precisely, as if their lunatic sweeping were a game of redwing roulette. You could smell orange, lemon, eucalyptus, and pepper trees, fields of poppies or alfalfa, and—at least once every trip—the recent discharge of some skunk, either generally outraged or murdered by a passing automobile. There was, I have to admit, too much of that for my taste, the sight of the poor, smashed blobs of creatures who had risked the passage from one foraging ground to another across an asphalt strip that roared with incomprehensible monsters.

Yet not even those little deaths could spoil the magic of our expeditions, for there was a countryside of charm, space, and variety in that part of Southern California once. Its towns and cities had not yet coalesced like some particularly virulent biological culture, and its air was not fouled by what Wallace Stegner has called the "taint of technology" (it was not until 1946, remember, that the citizens of Los Angeles recognized, or admitted, that they had an occasional problem with their air; they called it smog). From Colton to Riverside, the little two-lane highway cut through acres of orange trees that filled to the brim nearly every flatland and hollow in sight. Riverside itself retained its small-town, pseudo-Mediterranean style, with tall, fat palm trees and "Spanish" homes and businesses with red tile roofs. In fact, the whole downtown section of town through which we drove appeared to be variations on a theme established by the Mission Inn, Riverside's still famous hostelry of turn-of-the-century vintage.

Beyond Riverside, orange trees gave way to dairy pasture, vineyards and alfalfa fields, and the highway became a kind of embryonic freeway, its center strip planted with pepper trees and its shoulders with wind-breaking eucalyptus. At Corona, a hamlet whose only visible distinction was a circular thoroughfare used as an automobile race track in the 1920s and 1930s, the road curved into the slopes above the little canyon of the Santa Ana River, our region's barely legitimate claim to a respectable stream. Near home, the river was often no more than ten or fifteen feet across and a few inches deep, and in late summer it sometimes disappeared altogether. But in the canyon it had cut from the warm brown hills southwest of Riverside, it rattled along at a width of perhaps fifty feet and a depth of one or two feet. I have since seen genuine rivers, and know now that the Santa Ana was little more than an ambitious creek, given a stature it did not deserve by its presence in a nearly riverless land—as a small man would be considered a giant in a country of midgets. Still, it was quite sufficient to breed in me huckleberry visions of rafts and pirates and adventuring, particularly on those occasions when we stopped to picnic on its sandy banks beneath the shade of cottonwood and poplar trees.

After leaving Santa Ana Canyon, we would slice through orchard after orchard of the trees that gave Orange County its name (and, once, its reputation—but that was when there were more orange trees than people). At or near Tustin, my mother would announce that she could smell the sea. I always seconded this notion, although I never once smelled anything but orange trees. We would then be a good thirty miles from the ocean and how her nose managed to sift out the smell of iodine and salt I never knew, but there was no mistaking the sincerity of her mighty sniffs and exclamations of delight.

By now, the minutes were beginning to stretch intolerably. The games of out-of-state-license-plate-spotting and automobile identification had palled, and fidgets, squirms, whimpering, and pointless giggling emanated from the back of the car. "Are we there yet?" and "How much longer?" tumbled from impatient lips. Even the dog, getting into the mood of things, would begin to scrabble about, jumping on laps and slurping out indiscriminate licks. My father would tolerate all this for as long as fifteen minutes before resorting to a technique I am sure all fathers have utilized from time to time. He would suddenly pull to the side of the road, stop the car, and twist around to face us wordlessly. With one hand on the wheel and one long arm stretched across the back of the seat in readiness for instant deployment, he would give us all a look of such baleful menace that the tittering and wrangling would fade immediately. He would hold the pose and the silence for a very long moment before turning, starting the car, and returning to the highway. I can't remember whether he ever actually used the back of that hand on any of us; he didn't have to.

The village of San Juan Capistrano is widely noted for its crumbling, flower-draped mission, founded in 1776, and for its swallows, which return to the mission each year on or about St. Joseph's Day—a phenomenon that has inspired two or three hundred trembling little poems and at least one very bad song over the past couple of centuries. I couldn't have cared less about any of it, for the town's only importance to me was the fact that it was the final landmark between us and the sea. Two miles dead west of town, we would come to the Coast Highway and a decision: should we drive five miles to the south for San Clemente State Park, simply cross the highway for Doheny Beach State Park, or turn north for Salt Creek Beach? San Clemente had the best swimming among the three and Doheny lay in the shadow of Dana Point; both had much else to recommend them, including blockhouse rest rooms with showers, individual water faucets, sturdy tables and benches, rock-lined fire pits, and even a few fireplaces. Yet each was sealed off from the sea. The campsites at San Clemente were high on a bluff and a good ten-minute hike from the beach. Those at Doheny were separated from the sand by an asphalt parking lot fifty yards wide; there may have been more exquisite forms of torture than being forced to cross that thing in your bare feet in the middle of a summer day, but none occurred to me. (Wearing shoes, even to keep your feet from being parboiled, was, of course, unthinkable).

Salt Creek Beach lacked the amenities—unless one could include two pairs of sagging green outhouses that sang with flies and four or five widely-scattered water faucets as amenities. There were no firepits, save those you dug out of the sand, no benches, no tables, and most definitely no showers. But it had something better—the sea itself. Most of the campsites were strung along a thin gravel road that ran two or three hundred yards between crumbly sandstone bluffs and the beach. The campsites themselves were on the sand, so close to the water that at high tide the dying waves whispered only a few feet away. Unlike Doheny and San Clemente, where park officials assigned you a numbered and artfully plotted campsite, the people who ran Salt Creek Beach evidenced disdain for formality. After payment of a fee, the process of selection possessed all the qualities normally connected with the concept of squatter's rights: you grabbed a piece of sand of whatever dimensions satisfied your territorial imperative, set up camp, and held your ground against all comers. Fortunately, at Salt Creek Beach there were few challengers. Even in those unsanitized days before the Winnebago people started putting motel rooms on wheels, the sight (and smell) of those splintery outhouses was enough to strike panic into the heart of any normal American housewife. Those campers who remained in spite of the facilities accorded one another the sort of tolerance and quiet respect one mountain man might have given another.

Often enough to keep the memory of each occasion sharp in my mind, my mother and father chose Salt Creek Beach. The Yacht lumbering and groaning like an elephant, we would turn off the Coast Highway onto the camp's rutted gravel road. After stopping at the proprietor's shack at the head of the road to pay the fee and perhaps lay in a supply of beer and ice, we then crawled along beneath the bluffs until my father encountered a patch of sand that satisfied his nesting instincts. No one, including my mother, argued with him; this was his show.

His show, and his glory. I'm not at all sure that such moments were not the be-all and end-all of camping for my father, and that everything that followed was not anticlimactic. We would all tumble out of the car, and while the younger children scattered to play in the sand and let their feet be tickled by the littlest waves, my mother and I waited for instructions from my father. Whistling tunelessly, he would stand at the edge of the road and size up the situation like an architect surveying the site of a five-bedroom home. His calculations settled, he then backed the trailer and car into a suitable spot, disconnected the trailer, and propped its tongue on a wooden box. It would all come out then—the tent and tarps, the cots, the tools, the camp furniture, the dishes, the groceries, the boxes full of clothing, the Coleman stove and lanterns, the ice chest.

The tent, its back placed against the wind, was the first to go up. Its erection was a well-learned ritual in which I had a most satisfying role. After the tent was spread out on the ground in its proper position, my job was to help hammer in the long stakes that would hold it up and to tie pieces of rope to its numerous grommets. Then we would wrestle the thing into an upright position, and while my mother and I held desperately to the tent's center-poles, my father raced around its edges, pulling the ropes tight and securing them to the stakes. In a few moments, the tent could stand on its own while my father refined its structure, tightening and slacking ropes until it stood as neat and sturdy as an aluminum tool shed.

Into the tent I hauled and set up army cots and boxes of clothing as my father added on a room or two with his rope, his stakes, his bamboo poles, and his magic tarps. When done, the tent stood flanked on one side by the trailer, empty now but for the mattress and double-sized sleeping bag that served as my parents' bed, and on the other by an ingenious living-and-cooking area, complete with a sand-free (nearly) tarpaulin floor, a pair of folding card tables over which a large tablecloth had been spread, three or four canvas chairs (we usually ate in shifts), a cupboard improvised from wooden and cardboard boxes, and a Coleman lamp chandelier hung from a rope that was strung above the table—the whole complex surrounded on three sides by tarpaulin walls that kept out the wind and sun, and semi-blocked on its one open side by the Yacht itself, which doubled as an auxiliary cupboard and closet.

Given the materials with which he had to work, each of these summer beach camps was a little masterpiece of privacy and convenience, the epitome of a planned environment. Yet there was something of the dreamer and perfectionist in my father; he was never fully satisfied with any one of the camps and constantly seemed to be *at* them, adding a tarp here, taking one away there, moving the whole collection around to match the vagaries of the wind or sun.

The thing that irked him the most was the tent, which for all its size and weight was simply not quite big enough for five army cots, five kids, and the accoutrements that went with them, including clothes, sleeping bags, comic books and rock and-shell collections. Each year, the tent degenerated into a cramped little hovel that was my mother's despair, but there was little she or he could do about it. Even in the first golden age of the army surplus store, big tents cost big money.

My father brooded about this all of one winter, and by spring had come up with a solution: we needed a much larger tent. He couldn't afford to buy a much larger tent; *ergo*, he would *make* a much larger tent! Methodically, he drew up plans for a tent fifteen feet wide, twenty deep, and eight high (to ensure decent air circulation). There were to be no center-poles, guyropes, and stakes for this one, for it would be a nearly perfect rectangle built on a framework of standard water pipe which he would be able to pick up at a bargain rate (he knew someone who knew someone); it would assemble and disassemble through a system of flanged baseboards and connecting joints which he carefully sketched out. The covering for the frame presented a special problem, for it had to be light, water-resistant, and sturdy enough to withstand being hauled around and about; it also had to be of a single piece, with no cracks to let in the wind. The answer was an entire bolt of material that resembled oilcloth, which he found in the reliable army surplus store. Made of some kind of ancestral plastic, the stuff was a mot-tled green in color and may have been designed for purposes of camouflage during the then recent unpleasantness. In any case, it was light and seemed strong enough.

The project went on for weeks. While my father super-vised the clandestine measurement, cutting, and threading of his pipe (done without visible authorization in the mechanical department of the shop where he worked), my mother tackled the ghastly job of cutting and sewing all that material into a form the size and shape of a small house—all of it on her venerable foot-treadle Singer. Near the end of the task, there was so much material crammed into her bedroom that you could find out where she was only by the steady thrumming and clickety-clack of that old sewing machine.

Between them, they did it, somehow, and on one hot, still afternoon in late spring they tried it out. The framework went together with remarkable speed; my father had designed it well, and knew what he was about. The covering was then spread out on the lawn and one end of it carefully lifted over the top of the frame, slid over, then snugged down along the corners by the three of us. It worked; it worked, in fact, beautifully. The covering not only fit, it fit without appreciable slack. Inside, the tent seemed as still and huge as a cathedral, as mysterious as a cavern. It was an enormous success, and was left there in the yard for several days, perhaps to impress the neighbors, perhaps to see if it did not collapse from some unsuspected weakness.

The tent did not collapse, and it was broken down and taken with us on our next camping trip. My father selected our spot with even more care than usual, since our territorial needs were now greater. Then we went through a new tent-ritual. Once again, the framework went together quickly, and in less than ten minutes it was ready for its cover, which was spread out on the sand according to plan. But my poor father had not taken into account the intensity of the wind, which caught at the cover and billowed it like an immense parachute every time its end was lifted toward the frame, whereupon all three of us had to throw ourselves on it and wrestle it back to the ground. Time and again, we tried, with no success. Finally, his face growing tighter and redder the longer we worked at it, my father bundled the whole mess in his arms and with a mighty heave threw it on top of the frame, then leaped and caught at an edge of it and worked it part-way over one corner. Three more leaps, and he had a beginning.

It was hopeless. As we inched the material down the frame, the wind slapped at it viciously. One by one, my mother's painfully-fashioned seams began to give. Little rips became large rips, became tears, became mighty rents. Finally, we were reduced to helpless spectators as the wind battered our great tent to shreds. My normally reticent father extended his arms and shouted "Oh, God-DAMN-it!", following this with a string of magnificent oaths that commented on the perversities of the human condition, his own stupidity, and the parentage of the wind itself. Then he began to laugh, and we all laughed, clinging to the nearly-naked frame while the remnants of the tent flapped in the wind like pennants in a losing crusade.

That was my father's first and last venture into the world of Abdul the tent-maker. Thereafter, he contented himself with making do with what he had, year-after-year patiently building his little homes away from home, his little enclaves, his little fortresses against unknown perils, his little self-contained worlds on the edge of the sand where the sea muttered its ancient thunder, calling, calling.

Mysteries

MORNING: You had no way of knowing precisely what it was that woke you, whether it was the moist touch of wind laced with fog, the sound of the surf or just the peevish squawk of gulls as they flocked for breakfast. Whatever it was, you woke suddenly, like a businessman in a hotel room in a strange city. For a while you lay in the folded warmth of your sleeping bag and contemplated the day, while your dog, who had squirmed in with you at some point during the night, grunted comfortably as you squeezed her closer to you. If the day was typical, it would be about six o'clock in the morning. The top of your bag would be beaded with moisture, and overhead you would see the dank, gray clouds of overcast marching off toward the horizon like a series of lumpy, upside-down hills. Beneath the clouds, the slate-blue sea moved like oil, shrugging itself into halfhearted waves that dribbled quickly into foam, collapsing more with a sigh than a crash.

If the tide was out, as it often was, you did not lay in the bag for too long, for there would be things to see. Flushing the dog out, you wriggled into your blue jeans and sweat shirt, which had been tucked into the foot of the bag the night before to keep them warm and dry. You then tiptoed ever so quietly into the camp and grabbed your sand bucket.

In their trailer-bedroom your mother and father made a single great lump from which emanated a duet of murmurous snoring. From the tent where the rest of the family lay, there came no sound at all. They would all be good for another two or three hours, and you sneaked back out of camp and ran—raced—toward the exposed rocks and tide pools at the foot of the small point that lay perhaps a mile away.

You ran, dog at your side, not just to keep warm or for the simple joy of it, but because you wanted to take advantage of every secret moment of this time. Your parents had not forbidden these unsupervised expeditions; they simply did not know about them, and you wanted to keep it that way. God knew, it was dangerous enough a business, clambering barefoot over rocks polished by centuries of beating surf, made slick, smooth, and wet. One slip, and you could break an arm or leg, or even crack your skull. And if you were injured as far out on those rocks as you frequently ventured, you could lay immobilized until the tide returned and the sea washed your body away—and no one to know where you were. If you thought about it, it could all be pretty frightening—but of course you did not think about it. Your step was sure and unhesitant, your confidence boundless, your good luck remarkable.

And it was worth it, for this rocky landscape, stripped of the sea which kept it hidden for most of the day, vibrated with a secret, mysterious, unimaginable life that creeped and crawled in its pools, its dark nooks and crannies, like a population straight out of dream. Where else but out of the mists of dream could a hermit crab have been spawned? Barely an inch in length, he scrabbled and lurched among the rocks, seeking an unoccupied shell to inhabit; without it, he was a pitiful, helpless creature, his pink lower body curled under his torso like a tiny coil of rope; with it, he lurched along as before—quite as helpless, but at least granted the illusion of security. Starfish, too, were dream-like, inching through life on those impossible arms, changing colors to match their surroundings, their mouths a tiny slit in the bottom center of their bodies, where mouths had no business being. And more: crabs, pink ones the size of dinner plates with pin-

56

cers that could hurt, if not maim; mottled yellow ones as broad as the palm of your hand, little sand-colored ones no larger than your thumbnail; mussels and sea-snails clustered on the sides of rocks, extensions of the stone itself, immobile, hiding from the light, waiting for the return of the tide and their real world; an occasional landlocked ray trying to hide itself behind a rock in a tide pool and once in a while a smelt or a rock fish, or a gang of herring that had become similarly trapped; nearly invisible sea worms that squiggled along the bottom of pools like miniature snakes; and, most wondrous of all, the rainbow-colored anemonies, half-animal, half-flower, lurking in rock crannies with poison at the heart of their beauty. Over it all the ubiquitous gulls wheeled and screamed, small shadows of death that harvested what they could of that abundance of life.

You were entranced, utterly. Leaping from rock to rock, tide pool to tide pool, you poked and probed and watched everything you could watch. Lying on your belly at the edge of a particularly rich pool, you would be driven by the small boy's insatiable need to know, to understand, to experience—in short, to meddle. You would take out your little tin shovel from the sand bucket and use it to stir up a sleeping ray, if you could reach him. You would use it to stroke the petals of a crimson anemone, shuddering as the petals convulsed in an attempt to draw the shovel into its maw; thus you discovered that beauty could be a trap—a very large thing to learn at so young an age. You would seek out a large crab and toy with it until in its rage and fear it gripped the shovel firmly. You would then lift it out of the pool and dump it in your bucket, captured, helpless to escape the mindless cruelty of your curiosity. For you it was a game, for him a death struggle.

No matter how often or how long you visited this secret world, the potential for surprise was never absent—and it could sometimes be a large surprise, indeed. Once you discovered the body of a sea lion stranded on the edge of a tide pool far out among the rocks. You came upon it suddenly, unexpectedly, while crawling over the lip of a rock, and at first you thought it was alive. But no: the gulls had already been at its eyes. It was a huge mound of blue-black flesh, perhaps six or seven feet from nose to tail. You poked at the still resilient flesh with your shovel—gingerly, and a little fearfully. This was not your first dramatic encounter with death; after all, you had watched gulls hammering and picking at still-living crabs, a grisly and unforgettable spectacle. But never before had you realized the sheer power of a force that could destroy even this human-sized creature, leaving it to be picked at by gulls and crabs and whatever other scavengers there were who did the sea's bone-cleaning. To stand too close to it was to stand too close to your own end. You left it finally, left it for the sea that would reclaim it in a few hours.

Perhaps it was nothing more complicated than your stomach-clock sounding an alarm for food, but you always seemed to know when it was time to head back to camp. You dumped whatever creatures you might have in your bucket back into their tide pool and scrambled back across the rocks to the beach where your dog would be waiting (she possessed no measurable interest in tide pools or slippery rocks). Running along the beach (when did you not run?) you stopped now and then to scoop up a few shells, for you had to have some reasonable excuse for your long absence. *Where in the world have you been? Shells,* you could say, holding out your bucket. *I've been collecting shells.* The answer would suffice, for there was neither danger nor mystery in shell-collecting.

Mystery and danger were the very elements of a small boy's life then—certainly the elements of this small boy's life. A ten- or eleven-year-old-boy is the essential Romantic, a creature riveted by wonder most of the time, driven by the need to challenge the very heart of life the rest of the time, a confused and confusing mix of Don Quixote, Tarzan, and Neil Armstrong. Parents sometimes mistake his dreamy-mindedness for stupidity, his dare-devil antics for willful attempts to gray the hair of his elders. Not so. He is simply doing what his genes have programmed him to do, which is to learn the mystery and test the danger of life. Most of us get over all this, sooner or later; we acquire wisdom and caution, become bank managers or real estate salesmen or book writers, ultimately reaching that point in life when we are certain that all the mysteries have been learned, all the dangers tested. Others are not so fortunate, but they are to be pitied, not censured.

There was both danger and mystery enough in my world by the sundown sea—more than enough, more than could be learned, or tried. Take the mystery of the Sound, for instance. I have only heard it three times in my life, and those three times when I was a boy, but the memory of it has not diminished since, and I think I will be remembering it when my nerveless fingers are plucking at my last coverlet. The first time was pure accident, as discoveries usually are. Involved in my usual afternoon wave-chasing, I selected a towering devil of a wave to ride; it may have been twelve feet or more from base to crest, and definitely was not the sort of wave to try to ride. I realized my mistake almost immediately, but even then it was too late to do anything about it, for I was caught in its curl and would have to ride it out. The lip of the wave curved over my head, and for one brief instant I found myself in a long, green, transluscent tunnel that stretched forty or fifty feet on either side of me. That moment was when I heard the Sound, a high, hollow, almost metallic keening that cut through the outside roar of the surf until it was all that *could* be heard. It seemed to come from a great distance, like a cry out of the ancestral night, then swept over me and moved on just as the wave seized my helpless body and plunged it through the water and into the sand, where I gouged out a good-sized trench. The Sound could not have lasted for more than two seconds, but when I finally surfaced I was certain that I had been privileged to experience one of the essential mysteries. I tried again and again over the years to re-create the circumstances of that moment, but was able to do so only twice, each time as much by accident as by design. I suppose the phenomenon could be explained away by various acoustical laws having to do with decibels and the Doppler Effect, but I remain as convinced today as I was then that I had heard nothing less than the voice of the sea itself.

There were other things to know, less intense, perhaps, but no less wondrous in their own right. Not far from the point where the rocks and the tide pools lay was the canyon that Salt Creek had cut into the bluffs on its way to the sea (it was no more than an outsized gulch, of course, but it served my purposes to think of it as a canyon). Salt Creek was just a trickle by normal creek standards, but this was sandstone country—even the soil was little more than well-packed sand—and the canyon it had cut into the bluffs was deep and narrow and dark, running perhaps two hundred and fifty or three hundred yards back to the Coast Highway, and filled with a strange mix of coast chapparal, ice-plant, scotch broom, wild mustard, and occasional clusters of iridescent ferns in little dells where the creek had formed pools. And there were caves. The first time I ventured into the canyon, I counted seven open caves, ranging in size and shape from a niche-like hole that could barely shelter a child to a commodious little cavern that could have held half-a-dozen adults or more. How they got there I had no idea, whether carved by wind and weather, by Indians (although I found no bones, no skulls, no pottery shards to suggest it), or by those who followed. I immediately peopled them with all manner of types from my imagination, not excluding pirates, and fancied myself the first person to see them in generations.

I was wrong, a fact I learned in the last cave I entered. A medium-sized one with a nice sandy floor, it could have held two people in considerable comfort. It had held two people, in fact, and not very long before. They had not been playing pirates, I knew, for they had left something behind. I knew what it was. I knew when it was normally used and something of why it was used, and even had a primitive grasp of how it was used. But the existence of such things had always been a matter of rumor and speculation before; this was real, tangible, *right there*. Flushed with guilt and wild surmise, I stared at it for a long time, while confused and indistinct images boiled in my mind. In the midst of these fervent meditations, it occurred to me that these people, obviously having found the cave to their liking, might decide to return. Any time. Terrified at the thought of being discovered in my discovery, I ran from the cave and down the canyon. It was a long time before I returned.

As anyone who has ever watched the adventures of Jacques Yves Cousteau (or even those of Lloyd Bridges) must know by now, one of the most compelling wonders of the sea is not what is on it or around it, but what is under it. I found some of that wonder in my tide-pool explorations, but only that part which the sea itself chose to reveal. To know it truly, you had to enter the undersea world without passport, and explore it on your own. My expeditions along these lines were fairly limited, I have to admit. It was not yet an age when the aqua-lung was standard equipment for weekend hobbyists (nor could I have afforded one, in any case), and I had to make do with the basics, which were pretty basic: one rubber face mask that always seemed to leak just a little, one pair rubber flippers that never fit quite right, one plastic snorkel which I never did learn how to use properly. This was skindiving just one step removed from skin, but it was enough to give me at least partial entrance into a world I could not otherwise have known, that dim, green world where light entered in slanting, mote-filled rays, where rocks that were gray or black in the sunlight took on a spectrum of shadings from some dark rainbow, where dangling kelp became a coral jungle, murky, tangled, and dangerous, where the bottom sand was impossibly white, impossibly smooth, where the commonest fish acquired a mystery and dimension that transcended everything you had always believed you knew about fish.

In time, I took possession of a spring-powered aluminum spear-gun, one of the most deadly-looking instruments man has devised since the invention of the cross-bow. As my mother took pains to remind me, it *was* deadly, capable of piercing the midsection of a fully-grown man at a distance of several feet—*under* water. I promised faithfully never to aim it at the midsection of a fully-grown man, or even a half-grown one, and with my face mask, my flippers, and my snorkel I entered the water as a Mighty Hunter of the Deep.

What a fraud that pose was. In the two summers I sported around with that speargun, I did not fire it once at any living target. It was not as if I had never killed fish before. I had killed hundreds. Standing at the gunwales of a deep-sea boat, I had cheerfully hauled in barracuda, shovel-nosed sharks, sand sharks, halibut, sculpin, and once —almost—a sea bass so huge it bent my rod double before carrying my tackle back to the deep. Sitting in a rowboat on a lake, I had caught sacks full of blue gill, crappie, sunfish, and bass. Tramping the bouncing stream of Bear Creek in the San Bernardino Mountains, I had put limits of trout in my creel. Leaning on the rail of the pier at Newport Beach during the no-limit seasons of the mackerel run, I had pulled in dozens of the shining, muscular beasts, then gutted them, cleaned them, and beheaded them with the aplomb of an Elizabethan executioner. No, I was a fully-accredited fish killer of no little experience.

But I could not kill a fish swimming under water, nor did I ever try. It puzzled me then, and it has puzzled me periodically since, although I think now that I may be close to an answer. It was not that I was incompetent, and therefore afraid to try my skill. I had practiced assiduously, and was good—well, adequate. It was not that the fish were beautiful, particularly (although they *were* beautiful, as only a creature in his natural environment can be beautiful). It certainly was not that I had an aversion to killing; I had done enough of that, God knows. It was a kind of fear, I think, the fear of an alien in a world that neither welcomes him nor understands him. I could be tolerated as an observer, perhaps, but the moment I chose to kill, or try to kill, I would have chosen to become part of that world, to accept it on its own terms, to be fully vulnerable to all the laws which governed it, unto death itself. And some part of me must have known, or suspected, that the attempt could destroy me, for it was not my world. It would never be my world.

So I did not kill fish under water. And in the process of

not killing fish, and questioning why, I must have gained a hint, however subconscious, of a very important truth: that the mysteries we explore in the world around us (or below us) very often turn out to be mysteries within ourselves, that the challenge to test and know is a challenge to test and know ourselves first, the world second. I came much closer to realizing this truth the day I climbed Dana Point.

My father and I and a friend and his two boys had been out in Dana Cove all afternoon, diving for abalone (paradox: I would strip abalone from their rocks with a tire iron, but I could not kill fish). After we had paddled back to the beach where our two families waited for us, my father's friend suggested that the five of us men (or so he called us) try climbing the old hand-and-knee trail etched into the leeward face of the point, which rose straight above us like a wall. I was then, and am now, terrified of any significant height, and the idea appalled me. I assumed that my father felt the same, since to the best of my knowledge, in my presence or otherwise, he had never climbed anything higher than a ten-foot ladder, solidly planted. Yet he accepted the idea, for reasons which I still believe were not entirely rational. The man who suggested it was his friend. The friend was blonde, brown, muscular, and agile, while my father was black-haired, red more often than brown, generally slender (although he filled out nicely in later years) and stiff in his movements when not in the water. The friend was a back-slapping extrovert, while my father chewed his meditative cud. The suggestion was unmistakably made as a kind of challenge, and I suppose there was nothing my father could do but accept it, pride being the heedless thing it is.

Normally, my mother would have raised holy hell at any such idea, and I looked to her with a hopeful heart. But she was a very smart wife, and knew when to shut up. She said nothing. The thought of objecting personally, myself, never entered my mind. How could I shame my father? We climbed Dana Point.

Possibly because I was the smallest of the bunch—and therefore the most easily caught in the case of a violent backslide—I was put at the head of the line, with my father behind me, and behind him the other two boys and their father. We had only about 130 feet to climb, but I never traveled so long a distance in my life. The first fifty or sixty feet were not so bad, for they were up a little ravine that was blocked off left and right as if it were a tunnel; I could see only ahead of me or behind me, neither of which views were particularly alarming. Then the ravine ended, and I ventured out on the surface of the cliff itself. This was not good, for the higher I climbed, the more a sense of proportion I acquired. Height developed real meaning, because I could look off the left edge of the trail and see below me the rocks and surf of the beach, which became smaller and smaller the more I scraped and scrambled up the cliff. At one point, perhaps seventy or eighty feet up, I looked over the side and saw my mother, who waved unenthusiastically, a pinched and worried look on her face. I froze momentarily, for I had never seen my mother from such a height. She was a doll, an ant, and I knew suddenly, inarguably, that I was going to fall. I only prayed that I might land smack on my head, to keep the pain brief.

"C'mon, Tommy, let's get going." Behind me, my father's face was as shriveled and white as I was sure my own must be. But behind him, the two boys waited impatiently, fearlessly, as brainless as their father who had insisted on this whole business. I moved on, somehow, knowing perfectly well that at any moment I would make a fatal slip, or the ledge would give way beneath me, or a monstrous rock would crash down on me from above, punching me into the abyss where the waves made spiderweb patterns on the sand.

Suddenly, before I knew it, I was at the top. Above and to the left of me was the little wooden observation tower. One more series of carved footholds and I was over the edge, standing safe in the middle of several square feet of flat ground. Behind me, my father popped over the edge with a relieved and only slightly hysterical laugh, and after him came the two other boys and their father, all laughing, as if they were ready to do it again. The idiots.

Standing there, both feet spread wide, the wind in my hair, looking down on the miniature cove, I felt huge, Olympian. In spite of myself, I had met my fear and survived it. I had come to a working compromise with one of my deepest personal mysteries, for I knew as I stood there that my fear had been a very real and reasonable one, and should have been respected. I did not regret climbing Dana Point; I may even have celebrated it. But I knew that I would never do it again.

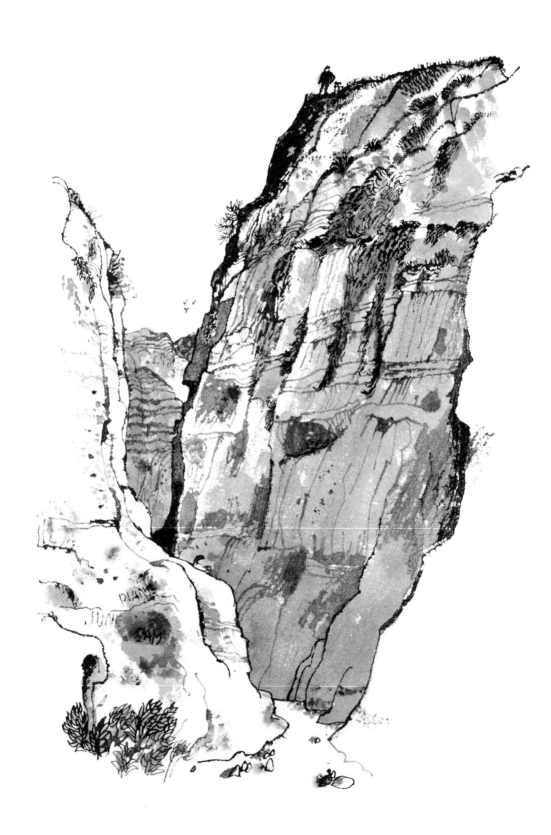

The Stranger

I CALL MY TYPEWRITER Black Maria, but it is in fact an Underwood Standard, *circa* 1938. Most of what I've written over the past ten years or so has been pounded out on its keys. That must amount to a couple of million words, if you throw in letters, notes to creditors, income-tax forms, and memos to various editors explaining my criminal neglect of deadlines. Maria shows the wear. Most of its keys have been fingered away to the point where the lettering has all but disappeared. It will not rewind its own ribbon, which has to be done by hand every twenty minutes or thereabouts, depending on how fast I'm writing. Rust spots most of its chromium-plated parts. Its Margin Release is erratic, its Back Spacer unreliable, its Tabulator a running joke. I don't mind. It is the only understandable machine I have ever owned, and I tinker with it, nurse it along, talk to it shamelessly. I am very fond of it.

But it is a willful beast. It has a way of taking over whatever it is I'm writing, giving it a form and direction I had in no way intended it to have. That certainly is what has been happening in these chapters, for I can see that my relationship with my father has been edging into center stage. Yet a book ultimately demands its own logic, and there is logic in this direction. If the shore of the sundown sea was the landscape in which I felt most completely at home, then the largest human figure in that landscape was that of my father. That was understandable enough, for it was only during such times that I really had much daily contact with him. His job kept him from home each night, and during the day he was a sleeping ghost in the house, a covered lump in whose presence we children crept as silently as it is possible for children to be. But each summer he emerged from his season of sleep to become once again a functional member of the family—and a tremendous force in my life. For it was my father, much more than my mother, I think, who governed the shape of my life. It was he I sought to emulate, his opinion which carried the weight of moral law, his approval or disapproval which pressed most heavily on my conscience, his love I most coveted—perhaps because it was so reluctantly expressed.

That may have been the key. There was a great fear in me that my father did not love me, could not love me. Something in him would not allow the easy, natural gesture of affection, the spontaneous hug, the reassuring touch, the tender word—all those things which my psyche demanded with the quivering passion only a child can generate, often to the point of explosion. All of these and more I did receive from my mother, but I could not rest easy in that abundance; perhaps in a perverse human manner, I placed less value on her love because there was so much of it, and that so available. In any case, I seized upon every rare expression of what my father kept hidden from me with his silence and his distance: our time in the sea together, when his face lit with a shared (but inarticulate) joy; his laughter, engineered with such calculation on my part; the occasional, undemanded, unexpected toy; the fishing rods built together, the fishing trips taken together, even the work done together. All of these I clung to like talismans, and I was right to do so, for they were all that I hoped they might be—the silent language of a real and abiding love whose intensity my unsubtle and insecure heart was a long time learning.

The learning came within the span of a single season in my bright landscape of the sea. It came with pain, as learning frequently does, and at first it brought me as close to despair as I suppose it is possible for a child to get.

On one of our early weekend trips to Salt Creek Beach, we had spent all day Sunday on one of what my mother usually called "jaunts"—somewhat aimless walking expeditions whose only visible purpose was to collect a few shells or rocks and to see what we could see. Over the sand we strolled, all seven of us (there were only five children then), past one beach after another, around one rocky point after another, wandering finally five or six miles before stopping for lunch and some afternoon swimming. Then we started back.

We had overextended ourselves, and the trip back soon degenerated into a trudging expedition. The heat softened our bones, sapped our energies. The thick sand and scattered stones, ignored earlier, became enemies to small feet, impeding or bruising them. The two youngest children began mewling in irritation and exhaustion and had to be picked up and carried by my mother and father. We were a hot, thirsty, tired, irascible bunch in a very short time.

With unerring instinct, I chose this instant to be my most petulant self, complaining that we had gone too far, that it was too hot, that I was thirsty, that the beach umbrella I was carrying was too heavy, and on and on in a whining monologue. I also insisted on climbing things, rocks mainly, that I was told not to climb, stubbornly ignoring my mother's warning that I was going to hurt myself, perhaps courting disaster as a matter of pure spite. Children are capable of such things—certainly I was. If so, I succeeded nicely, banging my knee on the sharp edge of a rock. Not a mortal wound, but genuinely painful, and I slid back to the sand awaiting the sympathy I so richly deserved.

I didn't get it. "I warned you, Tommy," my mother said coldly. "And if you break your leg, we'll leave you right here."

That, of course, was ridiculous, and since I had a way with smartmouth remarks, I said so: "That's just a lot of talk."

I don't suppose I will ever forget the look of icy rage that passed over my father's face at that moment (what parents tend to forget is that children do not). Shifting the child he was carrying to his left arm, he marched straight at me, high right hand cocked, while I stood as transfixed as a chicken mesmerized by a snake.

It was no halfhearted slap, but a full-bodied blow that

sent me spinning into the sand, my head ringing, my mouth full of grit. I lay there for a long moment, stunned—not just by the force of the blow but by the fact that it had come from my father. For it was the first time, to the best of my memory, that he had ever hit me. The physical discipline in our family had usually come from my mother, who believed that punishment should follow crime as soon as possible, and who had a persuasive way with switches and an occasional folded belt (not including the buckle, I should add), one or two blows from which were normally enough to convince any child of his basic wrongheadedness. Only rarely had I seen my father give a child even so much as a mild spanking, and never had he done so to me.

But now he had. Blubbering in pain, astonishment, and a profound conviction of Wronged Innocence, I leapt to my feet and went running down the sand, my knee throbbing, the salt taste of tears on my lips. Always ready to embrace rejection, I now had incontrovertible proof that my father not only did not love me, but might even hate me. How else explain his brutal behavior? Why else would he strike down an injured, helpless child for doing no more than speaking the truth? Well, that was all right. If he could hate, so could I. And so I did over the next several weeks, nursing my grievance with loving care until it bloomed in my innards like a hothouse orchid. I said nothing to anyone, of course, for I might have been talked out of my resentment, which was doubtless giving me much righteous pleasure. Most emphatically, I did not talk to my father about it, nor on the surface give him a hint of the bitter certainty I carried in my breast through most of that summer, a certainty that faded at times, but moved back into sharp focus whenever I consciously thought about it. I *knew*.

But I was not yet an adult, and therefore not quite capable of allowing this shrivelled knot of hurt and anger to sour my whole existence. I still had the world of sun and sand and sea with its swimming, its explorations, its real and fancied adventures, and when near the end of the summer we set up our annual vacation camp at Salt Creek Beach, I re-entered this much-loved world with my enthusiasm undiminished. At which point, the fates, or providence, or whatever, prepared to hand me the second part of a lesson whose first part I had been so sure was all I needed to know.

There was a steep slope, perhaps forty or fifty feet in length, not far from that little canyon whose caves held at least one real, and many imagined secrets. This slope was covered with a slick, rubbery blanket of ice plant and made an irresistible seat-of-the-pants slide (although it was hell on blue jeans), positively demanding that you push yourself off its edge and go slipping and bumping down with hilarious speed to land in the sand at its base with a satisfying thump. At dusk on the second day of camp, I did precisely that—but on the way down I felt a brief flicker of pain in my left calf, and when I hit the sand at the bottom I was startled to see blood filling my tennis shoe.

I was no stranger to my own blood. I had suffered the requisite number of cut fingers, stubbed toes, and nose-bleeds of youth—but nothing like this. Lifting my pantsleg, I saw a three-inch wound from which the blood poured in a steady, pumping stream, more of my own (or anyone else's) blood than I had seen in my entire life, more than I have seen since. Whether I had encountered the lid of an opened tin can or a broken beer bottle, I had no idea, nor did I care particularly. I was obviously dying. I ran—or hopped—back toward camp, bellowing not for the sure embrace of my mother, but for the help of the father I had thought I hated. He met me halfway and scooped me off my feet, running with me to the tent where I was thrown on a cot and my pants stripped from my legs.

With a handful of towel, a white face, and shaking hands, my mother knelt at the side of the cot and tried to stop the bleeding and clean the wound at the same time. It was useless. By pressing down on the cut with great force, she was able to slow the bleeding a little, but the blood continued to pour down my leg in great gouts. The wound also hurt now, tremendously, each little gush of blood accompanied by a rending stab of pain, but I did not cry. I was too terrified to cry, for I could see my very essence leaking away while my parents could only stand by helplessly and watch it happen.

My mother wrapped a clean towel around my leg and

held it there tightly. It slowly turned red. "It's no use, honey," she said, looking up at my father. "I can't stop it. We're going to have to get him to a doctor."

The nearest telephone was up at the office-shack of the campground's proprietor, and my father left the tent at a dead run, doubtless wondering where in the name of creation he could find a doctor on a summer Sunday night. "You're all right, darling, everything's going to be okay," my mother kept muttering to me, convincing herself no more than me. The fresh towel was soon replaced by another, then another. I remember wondering somewhat vaguely how much blood there could be in my small body—and how long it might take to empty it.

"Goddamn doctors," my father puffed when he returned. "Most of them told me to take him way the hell up to the hospital in Newport. But I got one who said he'd meet us at his office in Laguna." He took my mother's shoulders in his hands, moving her back. "Here, let me hold his leg for a while."

Since my mother did not drive, a neighboring camper volunteered to take us into Laguna Beach. A bathrobe was wrapped around me, and I was bundled into the back of the neighbor's car with my father, my leg in his lap, a new towel in place, his hand holding it with an agonizing grip.

It was almost dark now. Lying on my back, I could see the street lights flick by us as we raced into town, adding to the eerie, lightheaded feeling that had come over me, as if I were floating in the trough of a wave. For the first time in my life, I was forced to consider seriously the fact of my own death—not as an abstraction, as on the day I discovered the body of the sea lion or the day I climbed Dana Point, but as a real, physical fact. That was *my* leg that had been laid open to the bone; that was my blood slipping away in such fearful, constant streams. I was suddenly very cold, very alone, and very, very frightened. Then I saw my father watching me as the light from the street lamps slipped across his face. In each brief flash of illumination, I could see such an expression of love that my heart exploded in me, and I cried. I cried out of pain and shock, certainly, but also out of regret for the hatred I had nurtured for so long, out of a speechless

72

relief, out of a love that welled up in me to meet his own—and out of a paralyzing fear that now, when I had found the proof of my heart's long searching, I would be taken from it forever.

Death would have to wait for a while. The doctor did indeed meet us at his office, plunked me down on an examination table, gave me a quick shot of novocain or something, and stitched up my gaping leg as straight and orderly as the seam in a pair of Levis. (Some time later, our hometown family doctor took a look at the handiwork and groaned. "Why do these silly bastards have to be so *neat*? This boy is going to have a terrible scar." He was right). He then laid on a bandage and wrapped the leg in enough adhesive tape to cover it like a cast from knee to ankle. "Keep him down," he said briskly. "Keep him down, and bring him in to see me on Wednesday."

Keep him down. God, what an unjust sentence that was. Our vacation had only begun, and here I was, forced to recline on an army cot in the tent while my brothers and sisters—as well as the other children in the campground—were free to run and swim as my betrayed young body ached to do. I must admit that for the first couple of days the deprivation was not so bad. In the first place, I was sick with pain much of the time, each throb of my stitched-up wound like a hammer in my brain. In the second place, I was fetched-to and fussed over wonderfully by my mother, and even my brothers and sisters expressed what they could of sympathy, as well as awe at the drama in which I had taken part. After the second visit to the doctor, however, the pain diminished rapidly, and I itched for mobility. Still confined, I brooded in self-pity only partially relieved by the fact that I was the uncontested center of attention—and I lost even that when my oldest brother managed to develop a painful ear infection (what a cheap trick!). My mother and father gave it up at that point, breaking camp two weeks early, bundling us all into the Yacht, and heading for home before any more disasters struck us.

73

That was the Summer of the Terrible Vacation, as it became known in our family history, and as the most permanently damaged party, I can't say I disagree with the description. I had suffered more physical pain than I had experienced before and had endured real fear; but, more, I had lost the best part of one boyhood summer, each one of which was precious, because there would be so few. Yet if I had suffered and lost a great deal, I had also gained something so large that it not only cancelled out all the rest but gave the remaining days of my youth a dimension of strength that has colored the whole fabric of my life.

All the days of all those summers are like one to me now. With a few exceptions, remembrance has telescoped experience, until the large and small events that occurred over a period of five or six years sometimes seem to have happened within the space of a single summer, or even one long, passionate day whose hours were crowded with the magic, mystery, and innocence of my entire childhood. I know better. I know that the years of which I have been writing comprise one of the longest and, in many ways, most important chapters of my life, but there is nevertheless a kind of sunny vagueness about them as I try to reconstruct them from the well of memory, a confusion of hours, of days, of summers, and above all an uncertainty concerning beginnings and ends.

What, after all, are the boundaries of childhood? Superficial logic would seem to demand that there be such boundaries, convenient brackets to lay at the beginning and end of a neatly defined period of our lives. I wonder. Infancy might be said to end and childhood begin at that point when we start accumulating a deposit of conscious memory, but it is much more difficult to determine where childhood ends, if we can determine it at all. I think perhaps we cannot. I think that every step in the process of learning is, in effect, a step away from the certitudes of youth, placing us closer to that time when the fact and not the faith of things will govern our approach to the world. Along the way, we lose the essence of childhood by inches, like driblets from a badly-managed bank account, until suddenly, and sometimes painfully, we at last realize it is gone. For those of us who are lucky the realization comes late.

Still, there are signposts along the roads of this pilgrimage, moments when we know we have accomplished a good part of the journey we cannot avoid. One such moment for me was the day I learned to identify my father's love, and in the long run it may have been the most important of all. But there were others, as well. The one that quickens my memory more than most, and which some part of me insists was the final segment in the journey from boy to man, took place in the summer of my fifteenth year, when I first experienced the desperate urgings of love. I met a girl there on the sands of Salt Creek Beach, and for two weeks was entranced. I pursued her blindly, only half-hoping she could or would accept me. Then one day, she did—and I, caught in the terror of the unknown, turned away from what she offered. This mystery was too much for me. She, furious, turned to another boy. I did a thing then which makes me cringe even now: I followed them one day to a hidden shelf of sand, climbed a shoulder of rock, and watched them. The boy and girl were on the sand together, wrapped in the same fearful excitement that had so terrified me. It was clear that he was not going to run from the unknown, that he would explore the mystery she demanded he share. But it was for them alone, now, and some vestige of self-respect caused me to slide back down the rock to the beach and run back before it was too late, before I saw everything, before I learned everything.

That is as good a place as any to leave him—me—that half-child, half-man, sturdy, weak, daring, fearful, running along his landscape of sun, sand, and sea, a landscape which would never again hold innocence and unquestioned joy for him, a landscape that would even be gone in fact as well as memory in a few years. He was running, as he always ran, but now he would never be sure whether it was toward something or from something. I can see him there. I can see him. But I will never know him again.

PART TWO

The Monsters of Time

Men and not monsters warp the bounds of Sea.
Yet may not thoughtless men still monsters be?
Not fate but men unlock
The energies of rock,
And to what ends?

——HOWARD BAKER

Gifts

OTES ON THE PASSAGE OF YEARS: Inexorably, I grew past my landscape of freedom, for that simple world held no answers to questions that grew ever more complicated. Adolescence assaulted me like a fever, and the problem of who and what I was could not be resolved merely by throwing my body like a sacrifice into the waves of summer. Unfortunately, I found no answers in any other of the landscapes that followed. I became a football star, of sorts, but that told me little more than that I was better at knocking people down than someone else might have been. I tangled myself in the requisite number of moist backseat embraces of double-date adventure, and once in a scruffy bordello in Mexico City paid my entrance fee into the Mystery itself, but learned no more of Woman than I had gained on the sands of Salt Creek Beach. I felt the first restless stirrings of the urge to write, but only rarely did this give me a sense of self. I passed through adolescence scarred with uncertainty, and worked my way through college with only the vaguest notion of what, if anything, I intended to do with my life.

I took a job as a newspaper bundler, working by night, writing by day—reams of short stories, poems, and three-and-one-half novels, not a word of them publishable by any known standards. I married and sired two children, probably in an effort to identify myself to myself: a man with a job, a wife, and children was somebody, was he not? I fretted, and wondered, and played at the realities of life. On those rare times that I returned to the sundown sea it was as a visitor, not a pilgrim. How could it have been otherwise? There was nothing there for me now, for the time when it could have made me sure of myself and at least one understandable world was behind me, never to be recovered. Finally, I abandoned it all, all of Southern California in fact, driven by no more certain an instinct than the conviction that change was, somehow, progress. I piled our unimpressive collection of household possessions into a rental trailer, bundled wife, children, and dog (not Buttons, now; wracked by age, that dear animal pinched out the end of her days in the house of my parents) into our 1953 Chevrolet sedan (no Yacht, this), and headed up the coast to San Francisco—Mecca to my embryonic writer's heart. There, I found another job as a newspaper bundler, continued to work nights and write days, and fumbled steadily and not entirely miserably toward whatever it was that lay ahead.

Then life came up and got me, as it has a way of doing. "Sooner or later in life," Robert Louis Stevenson once wrote, "we all sit down to a banquet of consequences." Pursuing my undefined yearnings, I had dragged wife and children along behind me like the tail on a kite. If the winds of my uncertainty had pushed me about, they had tossed them around quite as much, perhaps more, but I had not considered this, had not even imagined it. So, the consequences, shattering my numb complacency until it lay glittering in ruins at my feet like broken glass in candle gleam. There were days and nights and weeks of passionate horror so psychically devastating that I cannot write about them even now, but the details are unimportant, save this: during one stretch of this dark night of the soul, I had been kept awake for more than sixty hours. My nerves trembled like the strands of a spider web in the breeze. My ears seemed filled with cotton, my mouth would not make the words come out right, my mind floated and stuttered, my vision was vague at the edges, as if I were wearing goggles. I knew nothing with certainty except that I had an eight o'clock shift one night and had to sleep, or die.

I could not sleep where I was, so I got into my car and drove, blindly, desperately, without known destination. I crossed the Bay Bridge into San Francisco, whose skyline had once called to me the way the Emerald City of Oz had called to Dorothy; now, it mocked me with the reminder of my failure. I had achieved nothing in my move north, and now might see everything that was left destroyed. I crossed the city and curved south along Highway One, through Daly City, Pacifica, Rockaway Beach, and over the mountains into the San Mateo coast region. Somewhere south of Half Moon Bay, I pulled off the highway and parked the car on an asphalt strip that overlooked a long beach, which one of the several along that strip of coast I cannot remember. It was a weekday afternoon in the very early spring, and the beach was deserted. A bank of fog lay three or four miles out to sea, hanging low in the sky like a gray curtain, but on the shore itself the sun shone brightly, and only the light breeze carried a hint of moisture. I got out of the car and stumbled over a sand dune to the beach.

Slowly, I walked along the surf-line, its rhythms singing to me like a lullaby. I kicked off my shoes and carried them in my hand, rolled up my pants and waded through the ankle-deep froth of dying waves. Near the far end of the beach, I found a large rock that provided some shelter from the wind. I scooped out a hollow of sand, as I had done so often in my youth, rolled up my jacket for a pillow, and lay down. I was asleep instantly.

When I woke, the sun was slipping down behind the curtain of fog, and the wind had the bite of a dying winter in it. I put on my jacket and shoes and walked back to my car. I was stiff and cold, but I had slept, finally, receiving what Anne Morrow Lindbergh might have called a gift from the sea.

That short visit to a world I had almost forgotten did not straighten out my confused existence, nor erase the problems to which I had to return. Time and circumstance would take care of that. But it had given me a few hours of solace, had softened the hard edges of my pain. Having rediscovered that world, I returned again and again, not just to that stretch of San Mateo coast where I had slept, but to much else—the awesome landscape of the Big Sur coast, where the primordial hills of the coast range plunge four thousand feet to the curling sea; the rocks and twisted cypresses of Point Lobos and the white sands of Carmel; the mist-ridden sweep of beach at Point Reyes National Seashore and the rocky coves of Bodega Head; the black forests of Sitka spruce and stunted pine that cluster on the hills of the North Coast above the mouth of the Russian River and the towering stands of coast redwoods that grow right down to the edge of the sea in the mountains above Fort Bragg; even San Francisco Bay itself, which I had virtually ignored since moving north, became an object of my pilgrimage of rediscovery. I took an office in one of the pier buildings that thrust out from San Francisco's northern waterfront and became entranced by the ships that periodically berthed outside my office window, their names redolent of far places and far things: *Oriana*, *Spirit of London*, *Hamburg*, *Viking Star*, *Mariposa*, *Monterey*. I bought a houseboat across the bay in Sausalito, and commuted to San Francisco on the early morning ferry, the *Golden Gate*, becoming as sea-wise as the rest of her regular passengers, who could walk the length of her rolling deck with a full cup of coffee in one hand and a *Chronicle* in the other and not spill a drop. I acquired a new list of sea-bound landmarks to add to my kitbag of memories: Pescadero, Half Moon Bay, Rockaway Beach, Stinson Beach, Baker Beach, Inverness, Tomales Bay, Santa Cruz, Angel Island, Portuguese Beach, Jenner-By-The-Sea, Russian Gulch, Gualala, Mendocino City. . . .

Clearly, the sundown sea had re-entered the mainstream of my life. Yet I could not enjoy it now with the undemanding innocence of my youth, for I understood too much. I knew that the assaults on this rediscovered landscape were proliferating even as I learned to know it again. I knew that piece-after-piece had fallen victim to the speculator's itch or was threatened by the concrete dreams of highway engineers. I knew that power-generating plants had altered the local ecology of coastal waters, that upstream dams had interrupted the natural processes of sandmaking and that beaches all along the coast were steadily eroding as a result, starved of fresh supplies of sand. I knew that oil-drilling rigs had punctured the floor of the sea and tapped into the black treacle of California crude, and knew that too much of it had escaped the careful pipes and pumps of the drillers, oozing to the surface where it lay like a hideous rainbow, stinking of the ages. I knew that acre-after-acre of public beach had been sealed off, illegally, from access to the people who owned it. I knew that metropolitan sewer outfalls had converted swimming beaches into death traps and that agricultural effluents saturated with pesticides, alkaloids, and chemical fertilizers had poisoned estuaries, destroying the habitat of millions of birds and underwater wildlife.

I did not know yet that the planners and developers had put wealthy ticky-tacky on the bluffs of Salt Creek Beach and laid a parking lot for boats in the cove below Dana Point, but I knew that the citizens of Big Sur had been forced to marshal all their energies to keep the Division of Highways from jamming a multilane freeway through the ancient mountains that meet the sea there with incomparable drama. I knew, too, that the citizens of the San Mateo coast had just barely prevented the U. S. Army Corps of Engineers and the Division of Highways from perpetrating one of the most outlandish exercises in blind progress this or any other country has ever entertained. Looking upon the beaches and hills and farms of that bucolic stretch of shore—unspoiled in the finest sense of the term—these two forward-looking agencies had decided that the area could support a population in excess of one hundred thousand people. Having come to that conclusion, they assumed, therefore, that it bloody well *should* support such a population, and they set about trying to make it possible. The Corps of Engineers laid plans to build a dam on Pescadero Creek, creating a reservoir to satisfy the thirsts of these nonexistent thousands of people, and the Division of Highways devised a proposed freeway system so that they could have ready communication with San Francisco and the communities across the mountains on the bay side of the San Mateo peninsula. Again, the people most likely to be victimized by this massive boondoggle rose up in vocal protest and managed to truncate the slide rule fantasies before they were translated into reality. How long they could hold the landwreckers back was another question; neither the Corps of Engineers nor the Division of Highways was notable for the grace with which it yielded to public pressure, and though the plans for each project were shelved, they were not burned.

As I explored the coast I had come to love again and learned more than I cared to know about the sundry idiocies to which it was subjected, I became convinced that of all the conservation issues then on the docket in California, the protection of this coast was paramount. California was simply inconceivable without her coast. Not only was it the dominant geographic fact in the state, stretching some 1,200 miles in actual shoreline from Oregon to Mexico, its existence was in a real sense the very definition of California's meaning. "Know ye that on the right hand of the Indies there is an island called California, very near the Terrestrial Paradise," a Spanish novelist had written at the beginning of the sixteenth century. He was outlining a country of myth, a country that did not exist by land or sea, but both the name and the sense of what he wrote became part of California's life. She *was* an island, separated from the rest of the continent by the barrier of the great wall of the Sierra Nevada in the north and the lethal sweep of deserts in the south. Like any other island, she was discovered and largely settled from the sea, and for most of her life the sea was the avenue of her commerce and communication with the rest of the known world. For more than four centuries, the smell and taste of salt spray flavored the history of this state. It was her single most permanent legacy, and one of her most beautiful.

To lose this coast to the machinations of engineers and real estate speculators was unthinkable, and I added my own voice to the thousands which began clamoring for some means of protecting what was left. Bills were formulated and introduced into the state legislature, whose members were apparently unconvinced that the people really cared a damn about what happened to their coast. Over a period of several years, no bill having to do with the planning and control of coastline development ever slithered out of the hands of one committee or another and went to the floor for a vote. Finally, in frustration and anger, conservationists took the question directly to the people. In the spring of 1972, a petition was circulated to place the matter of coastline legislation on the ballot as a referendum. The requisite number of sig-natures were obtained, and in the elections of November 1972, Proposition 20 was offered to the citizens of the state for a decision. Under its stipulations, a commission would be established to approve, disapprove, and watchdog all forms of coastal development, from housing projects to nu-clear power plants. Unsurprisingly, it was vigorously op-posed by a wide spectrum of real estate, public power, municipal, state, and federal bureaucratic interests. It passed by a stunning majority.

The passage of Proposition 20 was no small matter. It was the most comprehensive, detailed, and powerful piece of environmental legislation that any state or region in the country had ever considered, the single most telling illustra-tion of the profound shift that had taken place in the public mind in the previous ten years. The ecological movement had been labeled a temporary fashion by many—particularly those who would have gained by its failure—and when things like eutrification, effluent discharge, and photochemi-cal smog became subjects discussed by matrons at suburban cocktail parties the charge had some basis in fact ("Ecology," one irreverent wag wrote on the men's room wall of a San Francisco saloon, "is the last fad."). Yet the years of bom-bardment from television documentaries, magazine articles, newspaper stories, books, and political agitation had pro-duced something important. After more than a century of mindless worship of the growth ethic, the people of Califor-nia had confronted the monolith of progress with a single word: Stop. That is not faddish. That is revolution.

The passage of Proposition 20 was something else, too. It was an act of recognition and testament—a recognition of failure and a testament to hope. Like me sleeping out my exhaustion on that strip of beach in San Mateo County, the people of California had rediscovered the value of this sea-bound landscape, this golden shore, and had given it the only gift it was in their power to give—protection.

The Birds That Wept

A S I HAVE MENTIONED earlier in this book, my involvement with conservation has largely been an intellectual one, a matter of words more than feeling. I was asked once to testify before a genuine government agency on the matter of coastline legislation and did; and once I even presided nervously at a news conference on another conservation problem. But I have by no means ever been an activist in the sense the term is normally understood. Nor am I much for deep-breathing ventures into the wilderness world of backpacks, one-burner Primus stoves, woodcraft, and survival techniques. An occasional camping trip along the lines of those of my youth (although I am not nearly so good at the mechanics of it as my father was) is about as close as I have ever come to inflicting myself on an innocent Nature. Hiking depresses me; mountain-climbing terrifies me.

I don't feel particularly guilty about all this. One does not have to sleep alone under a tree in wild country, it seems to me, to appreciate the value—no, the necessity—of wilderness as the single most inescapable reminder that we are natural creatures living in a natural world, no matter how close to the angels we may believe we are, no matter what we try to do to that world with plastic and concrete. For me, at least, it has always been enough to know that wilderness is there to be convinced that it should always be there, as the essential part of what Wallace Stegner called "the geography of hope" in his classic wilderness manifesto. Neither does it seem to me that one must necessarily walk a picket line, call door-to-door, distribute leaflets on a city street, formulate legislation or lie down in the path of a bulldozer in order to demonstrate concern. Someone, after all, has to state the problem, and we also serve who only sit and write.

That said, I have to admit that there is a danger of sterility in the purely intellectual approach to conservation (or anything else, for that matter). To avoid it, a man's mind needs to be nourished with the blood of anger from time to time, and that can only come when he is reminded that the problem is not only real, but personal. I gained a most valuable measure of anger that day in the spring of 1970 when I stood on Dana Point and looked down on the ruined landscape of my youth. I gained another on the winter day some eight months later when, for the first time, I heard the sound of birds weeping in sickness and fear.

The night before, I had been lost in one mystery novel or another when Joan called me shortly before midnight. "Have you been listening to the news?" she asked.

"No. I've been reading. Why?"

"They've had some kind of tanker collision in the Bay. I don't know the details, except that there seems to be oil all over the place and they're asking for volunteers in the morning. I'm going. Do you want to go with me?"

To my everlasting discredit, I hesitated. I had a full day of work ahead. Deadlines to meet. Bills to pay. Laundry to pick up. There were any number of reasons why it was impossible for me to go. But the urgency and determination in her voice would not be denied. Besides, some part of my mind told me, this was not Santa Barbara or West Falmouth. This was San Francisco Bay. *My* bay. "Sure," I said finally. "What time?"

"Early, I guess. Five o'clock?"

Five o'clock. My whole being rebelled at the idea. "Okay," I said. "I'll pick you up."

It was a morning to match disaster—cold, windy, overcast, heavy with moisture and smelling of fog. When I arrived in San Francisco, she was waiting for me, dressed in a pair of battered green corduroy pants tucked into the tops of

90

a pair of even more battered old boots, at least two sweaters, and her "furry," a thick outdoor coat with an imitation fur collar and hood. The combination made her look like Spencer Tracy in *Captains Courageous*. "Scoff if you will," she said, "but it's going to be wet and colder than hell. You," she added, looking at my ancient summer slacks, tennis shoes, and sweater, "are going to freeze your tail off."

"Maybe." She had a cardboard box with a small blanket in it. "What's that for?" I asked.

"The birds. You're supposed to wrap them in the blanket to keep them warm and carry them in the box so they won't hurt themselves fighting you."

The birds. Of course, there would be the birds. I remembered photographs from the oil spill at Santa Barbara in 1969. Not good to look upon. "What do we do with a bird once we've found him?" I asked as we scuttled as quietly as possible down her apartment stairs.

"Take it to a bird rescue center. According to the radio, they've got them scattered around the city."

Following the lead of regular radio announcements that reported on the areas most in need of volunteers, we drove down to the St. Francis Yacht Harbor on the edge of the city's Marina Green. In the gray ghost of morning light, the scene that greeted us was something perhaps only a Gustave Doré could have drawn effectively. The still water in the harbor itself shone with a dim, dirty glimmer like that of dishwater, and the outgoing tide had left rings of filth on the hulls of most of the boats I saw. On the stretch of beach that bordered the harbor's breakwater, a long line of shadowed pitchforks and shovels rose and fell against the slate sky with a kind of manic rhythm. Workers—many of them city employees, but many of them hippies and college students whose bearded faces and long hair, incredibly, were topped by bright orange hardhats—methodically pitch-forked hay into the water, let it soak, then raked it out and shoveled it into city maintenance trucks. The straw went into the water light and yellow; it came out heavy and black, matted with oil. The workers had been at it for a long time. They sweated and grunted with their loads of clotted hay and talked very little among themselves. The unearthly stench of petroleum hung in the air like a draft from the back door of hell.

We walked down to a small building where a group of volunteers, most of them young, milled around. The building was the harbormaster's office, converted now into a kind of emergency center. Leaflets explaining the methods of rescuing and caring for birds were passed from hand to hand, as were the addresses of several bird rescue centers. We waited with everyone else, waited for someone, somewhere, to tell us what to do. After several minutes, a bearded young man emerged from the office and announced that a couple of boatowners down at the opposite end of the harbor had volunteered to take their boats out on the bay in search of floundering birds. They needed crews, and in response hands shot up all around us. Blankets, towels, boxes, and jars of baby oil for bird-cleaning were handed out, and from somewhere numerous long-handled nets appeared. Loaded down with rescue equipment, we all trooped back to our cars and drove down to the other end of the harbor, eager to begin whatever it was we were to do. As it turned out, there were too many for the two boats. Joan and I were left behind. Except for our own box and blanket, we turned over our equipment and watched the boats off.

Superfluous, confused, and frustrated, we returned to the Marina Green and wandered up and down the walled edge of the harbor, watching the slick, gray surface of the water. After a time, she gripped my arm and pointed. "Wait a minute. Isn't that a duck or something?"

It was a coot, so tiny and low in the water that he was almost invisible as he paddled heavily around, apparently searching for a spot that did not crawl with oil. Slowly, with visible effort, he moved toward our side of the harbor.

"Can we get him, do you think?" she asked.

"I don't know. Maybe if he comes close enough I can wade out and grab him."

"We need a boat or something, I'll go look for one."

"Okay, I'll see what I can do from here."

While she went trotting off, I lowered myself down the wall to the rocks at its base. The coot was close enough now for me to see that it was nearly blind with oil. Even its beak was black with it. I rolled up my pants-legs and waded out to where the bottom dropped off abruptly. The water was a ring of ice around my knees and shone with a dull rainbow glow. I waited, shivering, since there was nothing else I could do. Surely driven by nothing more than an aimless instinct for survival, the coot drifted closer and closer to me, its beak open, apparently straining for air it could not get through its clogged nostrils. When it was no more than ten feet from me, I reached out my arm. Somehow, the coot saw me, or sensed me, and turned frantically, flapping its oil-heavy wings to escape what must have seemed an even greater danger than oil. Helpless and angry, I watched the bird until it was once more just a spot on the water. I waded back to the wall, where Joan stood waiting.

"I couldn't find a rowboat anywhere," she said as she gave me a hand back up the wall. "I guess they've all been pressed into service."

Even from a distance, it was clear that the coot had sunk even lower in the water than the first time we had noticed it. Quarter inch by quarter inch, it was sinking, and would drown soon. And all we could do was stand and watch it die. "Godamnit," I said, "let's go someplace where we can *do* something."

We tried. We drove up to the Cliff House and parked the car. After a cup of coffee at a nearby greasy spoon, I climbed over a fence, ignoring numerous no trespassing signs, and scrambled down the slopes to the rocky beach. She waited above, in case explanations should become necessary. For half an hour, I crawled over rocks and around the concrete foundations of the long-since destroyed Sutro's Baths, relics of a time when oil spills were either unknown or shrugged off as the inconvenient, but tolerable, price of progress. No birds. We drove over the hill and down to Ocean Beach, where we left the car in the shadow of the rickety, ghost-like roller-coaster of Playland-at-the-Beach. We marched slowly down the beach looking for birds. The foam of the open sea's breakers was a creamy gray sludge, and each wave left a tracery of oil on the sand, but we saw no birds, in or out of the water. After more than an hour of wandering, we returned to the car and switched on the radio. Linda Mar Beach, the radio announced. Volunteers were needed at

93

Linda Mar Beach, near Pacifica, some five miles down the coast. "Well, what the hell," I said. "We've tried everything else."

It was well past noon when we arrived at Linda Mar Beach, a two-mile curve of sand and surf on the coast below San Francisco, but the overcast still hung in the sky like a dark ceiling. We left the car on a bluff at the southern edge of the beach. Across a little meadow to the south of us a sideshow-sized tent had been erected as a bird rescue center, but it was crowded with people and obviously in no need of volunteers. To the north, there was a need. Scattered along the beach were black pools of oil, ranging in size from a yard or two across to huge deposits sixty or seventy feet in diameter. A raggle-taggle army of people was strung along the sand into the distance, doggedly working at the pools of oil in an attempt to clean them from the sand. It was a patently impossible job.

We climbed down the bluff. From a height, the oil pools had appeared liquid, but as we walked closer we could see that they were more like tar. Most of the hundreds of people who tugged and pushed and dug at the stuff were hippies, teen-agers, mothers, and children; one of the mothers explained to us that the schools in Pacifica and Linda Mar had been let out for the day, so that the beaches could be cleared of the oil which had been carried out of the bay and spread along the southern coast. At a point halfway up to the beach, we stopped, looked at each other, grinned a little foolishly, and dug in. There was nothing dramatic about this job, as there doubtless was in the act of rescuing birds. This was the crudest sort of barehanded labor, dirty, difficult, and exhausting. But it was good to be doing something at last, scraping up the oil with flat pieces of wood or simply scooping it up in our hands, carrying it to a nearby cardboard box or plastic bag, then helping to haul filled boxes or bags up the sand to a point above the tide line. When the boxes and bags ran out, the oil was carried a handful at a time and piled up in oozing mounds, half-sand, half-oil. At regular intervals, a monstrous three-axle dump truck with a crew of five or six strong young men crawled up the beach, stopping along the way to pick up the product of our labor. When the truck became mired in the sand, twenty or thirty people ran to help push it out.

Almost before we had noticed it, the sun broke through the overcast. Coats, sweaters, and shirts came off, and our cold sweat was warmed by the sun. Joan and I stopped once to look at each other. We were a mess. My tennis shoes and her boots had disappeared beneath a gummy layer of oil, and our pants were coated and streaked with it. I could see it in her hair and smell it in my own beard. Our hands and arms were black, our faces smudged. Nearby, a bare-chested teenager noticed our amusement, then looked at his own hands and arms and at his nearly spotless chest. He scooped up a handful of oil and rubbed it across his front, and apparently satisfied that he had created a kind of balance in his appearance, bent back to work.

Steadily, with God knows what manic energy pushing us on, we worked through the afternoon almost unconscious of everything but the viscous patches of oil-covered sand beneath our feet, the mounds to which it had to be carried, the truck into which it had to be lifted or shoveled. It was not until dusk that I can remember looking up from the work for any length of time. I noticed then that the hundreds of workers along the beach had dribbled away to dozens—for good reason, because, remarkably, the oil was almost gone. In the face of what had seemed to be impossible odds, the great pools of oil had been reduced to streaks and patches that disappeared even as I watched. There was no elation in us as we walked back down the beach. We were numb and mildly stunned, as a soldier must be when the sounds of war are replaced by the silence of sudden truce.

Rumor had it that there was food up at the bird rescue center. We climbed the bluff and crossed the meadow to the great tent, which glowed in the gathering darkness from the lamps within. Huge shadows danced on its walls. There was food there, right enough, spread out on a series of folding tables outside the tent. What it was, I cannot remember, but it was warm and filling and we ate. While we stood there with paper plates in hand, the call went out that another boatload of birds was being brought to the center and that more baby oil was needed to clean them. Without really thinking about it, I trudged back to my car while Joan went into the tent to offer her own services. I found a supermarket open a few miles down the road, and stripped its shelves of the last few large bottles of baby oil. When I returned, I gave them to someone who seemed to be in charge of such things and entered the tent in search of Joan.

It was a long tent, illuminated by a string of Coleman lanterns and ordinary flashlights strung from the ridgepole that ran the length of its roof. Along each side of the tent stood lines of people, Joan among them. Down the center were two long rows of boxes, perhaps as many as forty, and in the boxes were the birds, each of which was being cared for by a single person. Most of the birds were cormorants, grebes, terns, ducks, and coots, creatures more often on or under the water than above it, unlike the more fortunate gulls. All of the birds were sick with oil. With an indescribable tenderness, their attendants poured baby oil on them and rubbed them softly with cloths, cleaned out their eyes and nostrils with oil-coated swabs, held them to give them warmth.

The birds were crying.

I suppose it is ridiculous to say such a thing, but I do not know how else to describe the anguished, terrified piping that filled the tent, that cut through the thin, almost embarrassed murmur of human conversation. It was a constant, nerve-shattering song of despair in a language from another world, yet a language that even humans could understand. Like a litany it rang through the tent. *Why, why, why!*

Softly, slowly, as if in a hospital room, I moved to Joan's side. There were tears in her eyes. I knew what she was feeling, what every watching person in the tent had to be feeling. I felt it. I wanted, I needed, to hold one of these birds, give it comfort, give atonement, explain in a manner beyond words that this was not the way any of us, any of us in the world, had wanted things to be, that we knew it should not have been and must never be again. Even though I realized that not one out of ten of these birds would live after this night, no matter how much care was given, I yearned with all my heart to give them what little I could.

But there were more people than birds. There was no need for us here. Our hovering presence, in fact, was probably doing the birds more harm than good. We left, finally, returned to the car, and drove the dark miles back to San Francisco. If we talked, I don't remember. I don't think we had to talk.

As I write this, it is almost three years since that day and night. The oil has long since disappeared from the beach at Linda Mar and the shores of San Francisco Bay—except that portion that may have emulsified and sunk to the floor of the sea and bay to do unknown damage to the creatures which reside there. The bird populations have replenished themselves from their gene pools and still fill the air with wings. We were not undone that day and night, and it is easy to forget the likelihood of a recurrence. For myself, it is difficult to dredge up the memory of the frustration, filth, and exhaustion of our eighteen hours of searching and labor. But I have not forgotten the sound of the birds that wept. Nor do I wish to forget it. For my own sake, I hope I will be remembering it for the rest of my life.

Houseboat

T HE GREAT BLUE HERON has joined us again this morning. Its pipestem legs stepping along with a slow,
arthritic grace, its great S of a neck swaying with each
step, its bright, yellow-rimmed eyes watching everything
that moves, it strides up our dock until its daggered, eight-
inch beak is passing by the window of our dining area. It
stops then, and gazes with much intensity into the glass,
studying us as we sit over our coffee. Neither of us moves or
speaks, for fear of startling it. After a time the bird moves
on, the important business of looking for a fat sunfish up-
permost in its mind, but I'm sure it must wonder in these
brief moments of observation just what on earth such huge,
wingless creatures are doing out here on the fringes of its
world.

What we are doing is living on a houseboat.

This remarkable fact still gives me a start of disbelief
when I think about it, although I suppose it is no more than
the logical end of that moment when I rediscovered the sea
on the San Mateo coast. Next to residence in a sea-going sail-
ing vessel or in a house perched above the surf on the Big
Sur coast, I can think of few lifestyles more closely wedded to
the sea than that which I am living today—although, to be
perfectly accurate, I must point out that this is not exactly the
open sea. What it is is Richardson Bay, which is an extension
of San Francisco Bay, which is an *arm* of the open sea. Still,
we live each day with the rise and fall of the tides, and that
is as seabound as I am ever likely to be.

Getting here was no simple matter. It began when a friend of Joan's offered her own houseboat apartment for subletting for a couple of months. We took her up on the offer, and after no more than a month knew that this life should be our life. We began to houseboat-hunt doggedly, looking for a place to rent or buy among the hundreds that cluster along Sausalito's waterfront region. In the slick hands of real estate agents, we covered that waterfront. We looked at houseboats that were no more than floating tickytacky, as if one of the modern hovels that dot the hills in San Mateo had been hauled to Sausalito and placed on a hull. We could not stand them. We looked at an old tugboat which had been converted into an utterly charming version of a Mississippi steamboat, complete with filagreed railings and fretwork and dark, interior woods that had been fitted and polished by the hands of a loving craftsman. It was too small. We looked at a floating Moorish palace, a veritable mansion of a houseboat, with fifteen-foot ceilings, parquet flooring, an immense bubbled skylight, and a front deck with marbled pillars. The asking price was ninety-five thousand dollars. For weeks we scrambled over boardwalks and floating docks, poking our heads into windows, checking plumbing, bickering over prices, asking about leaks.

Finally, we found our houseboat sitting at the end of a long floating dock that thrust clear into the middle of Richardson Bay. The view from its front deck showed us a wide stretch of open bay over which Mount Tamalpais loomed like a miniature Fuji, stringers of fog slipping down its wooded flanks. The surface of the water was smooth as a ballroom floor, and if you closed your eyes the rumble of traffic crossing over the Richardson Bay bridge a mile away sounded like the muffled thunder of distant surf. About twenty yards from us, a flock of terns flicked and hovered over the water in search of herring.

The boat itself was larger than any we had seen since the floating palace, with a hull more than thirty feet in width and fifty long. The house was a simple rectangle about twelve feet in height. The portion of it that faced the open bay was almost entirely glass. Inside we found one huge room whose rear half had been partitioned into two bedrooms and a bath. The remaining half was given over to a living room and kitchen combination. In one corner, the huge mouth of a franklin stove gaped at us, and overhead four-by-twelve beams swept across the width of the ceiling. There was nothing elegant about it. The wood panelling was cheap and old, and seemed to be coming off its studs here and there. The partitions that set off the bedrooms were short of the ceiling by at least two feet, giving the interior a curious, unfinished appearance. The refrigerator in one corner of the kitchen was old enough to qualify as an antique, and the stove was a tiny four-burner. In the bathroom, the toilet gurgled uncouthly, and the shower was no more than a flexible hose. The water pressure was anemic, and the lighting system atrocious. The outside stairway which led to the roof was rickety, and on the roof itself stood a pair of crude sheds which sheltered the current owner's collection of racing pigeons. Altogether, the houseboat had the general aspect of something put together by a committee. It was big and ugly and homemade—and we loved it instantly.

Joan continued to poke around the house while the owner, the agent, and I circled in the ritual of house-buying. The asking price made my heart stop, but the agent gave me an owlish glance which suggested the owner could be persuaded to come down significantly. I grunted cynically at the claim of the pair of them that this was the only houseboat in the harbor that did not leak during the rain and made some pointed remarks concerning the inadequacy of the plumbing and potential heating problems—all of this designed to convince them that while I was interested, I was by no means sold. I'm not sure the pose was particularly effective, for as we left ("We'll have to think it over," I said brilliantly) I saw the agent and the owner exchange sly smiles.

Walking back to the car, Joan held my hand tightly. "Do you think we can do it?" she asked.

"I don't know," I replied. She had never asked me for anything before, and even now she would not do so directly. But the restrained yearning in her voice was unmistakable, and I knew that she wanted this dear, rustic, impossible houseboat as much as I did. My voice said "I don't know," but my heart was echoing my mother's words when she and my father had faced the question of the new car so many years ago: "We've *got* to do it."

We did do it. We borrowed and manipulated and bargained, and one day signed the papers that made it our own—ours and that of one of the few banks in the continental United States that ever made a loan on a houseboat. We spent nearly a week scouring and scrubbing and painting, and two days carrying furniture and box after box of household goods the one hundred and fifty yards out the narrow floating dock, which bobbed and weaved treacherously, especially over one last stretch of open water. By the time we decided the place was ready to be lived in—with approximately ten thousand things left to do—we were sore and exhausted. But we sat on the front deck that first evening and watched the sun splash color all over the sky above Mount Tamalpais. We listened to the cry of gulls as they slipped across the darkening water and felt the houseboat move gently in the breeze. We broke open a second bottle of wine and grinned at each other like idiots. We've been doing it periodically ever since.

We are well into our second year on the houseboat now, and still weighing the advantages against the disadvantages of this life. So far, the advantages have a heavy edge over the disadvantages—even though these are manifold and basic. Everything that enters or leaves the houseboat, from garbage to groceries to firewood, has to be carried on our backs or in our arms the length of the dock. This is not only inconvenient, it can be downright dangerous in stormy weather, when the dock bounces and twists against the waves like an obstacle in a Fun House. Never being particularly good on my feet under the best of circumstances, at such times, I have been known to spend a good five minutes negotiating the last stretch of open water between me and the fires of home. Neither of us has yet been pitched off the dock into the water, but we live with the possibility.

We are at the mercy of the elements in other ways. For one thing, the houseboat does in fact leak when it rains. I will not say that the owner and the agent lied to me about this. Rather, they obscured the truth in the manner of high-level presidential campaign officials. It is not the roof that leaks, you see, but the walls. If anything, wall-leaks are worse, for when a roof leaks you can at least place pans and bowls to catch the drips, but there is little you can do to stem the insidious seepage that oozes out from beneath the walls and by osmosis enters the very fabric of your carpeting. At such times, our life is not only on the water but *in* the water, and the dismal squish of our steps accompanies our every move. The only good to be found in it is that it gives us something to do with our old newspapers, for we lay them down, let them soak, bundle them into a plastic bag, and lay down fresh ones in endless sequence. I have been at work this past summer with a caulking gun, and soon will go about with a bucket of tar, but as our second winter approaches I know we face the prospect of once again living in a swamp.

Roof and even wall leaks may occasionally trouble the normal householder. The problem of mooring lines almost never does. With us, mooring lines are a matter of some concern, for the winter storms which assault this end of the bay can be vicious and damaging, with winds that approach and often exceed fifty or sixty miles an hour. The action of wind and wave puts a tremendous strain on lines, and this last winter two of ours snapped like so much thread. I was able to snug us back to the dock before the remaining two lines gave way, and it was just as well that I did, for if this 36,000-pound monster ever broke loose it would take half the boats in the harbor with it. This winter, I will have extra rope handy.

Part of the houseboat did in fact get away that winter. During one particularly stormy night, Joan went off to Oakland to care for her mother, and I wriggled into my sleeping bag in front of the fire, for both the warmth and the psychological comfort it provided. I lay there watching the flames and nipping at a bottle of sherry while the wind screamed outside and the houseboat rocked and groaned and

swayed, moving with more violence than it ever had before. Before drifting into sleep, I entertained the fantasy that I was in the fo'c'sle of a clipper ship caught in the Straits of Magellan. Reality interrupted romance some time later, when I was wakened by a horrendous crashing noise from the roof, followed by a tremendous splash to the left of the houseboat. My heart pounding, I threw on some clothes and went out into the rain, where I discovered that the wind had torn one of the old pigeon shacks from its foundation, shoved it clear across the roof, and thrown it into the water, taking our television aerial and part of our chimney with it. It floated out there now like a battering ram, threatening neighboring houseboats. I jury-rigged a grappling hook from the curving metal handle of a paint roller and stood on the deck for an hour in a sea of wind and rain trying to haul the shack in. I finally succeeded and tied the thing to the side of the houseboat, where it remains today, rising out of the sea at every low tide like the creature from the black lagoon, curtains of greenish-gray algae hanging from its frame. It is too big and heavy to be pulled from the water and too well-constructed to be broken up; I suppose it will be with us forever.

Always impractical, usually inconvenient, and sometimes uncomfortable, houseboat living does indeed have its disadvantages. But they are nothing compared to what it offers of peace and privacy, of solitude and simplicity, of the joy of being so close to a natural world that you can sometimes convince yourself that you are part of it. Each day of life on the houseboat is like a day spent on an island where you can for a time delude yourself into believing that you have escaped the caterwauling demands of the twentieth century. Even the storms of winter, sweeping down on you from the hills of the Coast Range, present a challenge so elemental that all other problems and pressures are diminished by comparison, becoming almost as insignificant as they should be, as they would be if the universe were in better order.

This is a separate world, this world of the houseboat. And its proper inhabitants are the birds. I have never been much of a birdwatcher before, but I am now. It would be foolish not to be, for they are so much a part of this world that to ignore them would be like refusing to consort with the natives while living in a foreign country.

You begin with the gulls, the ubiquitous gulls, who are so numerous, so wily and indestructible, so greedy, ill-tempered and individualistic (and never mind what *Jonathan Livingston Seagull* says) that they cannot help but inherit the earth. I know them by sight now—the herring gull, with its mottled gray feathers and faded beak, the common western gull, with its orange beak, white head, and smooth gray wings, and Heering's gull, a rather rare type for this area, with a bright red beak, black feet, and black-tipped wings. No matter what the variety, the personality flaws of the gull are massive and unrelieved. Tough and mean, they are sur- vivors, these birds. They can and will eat anything, and threaten to kill one another for the privilege. If they were human, the gulls would be the bankers and brokers and literary agents of the world.

I like the terns better. While they do not fly so beauti- fully as the gulls (let us give Jonathan his due), they are too busy to become mean-tempered. A gull will gorge itself, then sit for hours practicing the art of digestion. The tern has no time for leisure, for it is caught up in a constant cycle of feeding and flight, burning up prodigious amounts of energy in the very act of feeding. Wings beating furiously, it will swoop and hover over the water for seconds at a time like a great hummingbird, then fold its wings and plummet down with a tiny splash, only to rise again instantly with or with- out a herring or fingerling smelt in its craw, and repeat the whole procedure. When darkness finally drives it from the water,the tern must be exhausted.

I have already mentioned the great blue heron, surely the most spectacular member of this world. Stately and de- liberate, this bird is the monarch of all it cares to survey; not even the gulls will challenge whatever territory it takes as its own fishing-grounds, for the pointed beak that tops its whip-like neck is as lethal as an Italian dagger. The heron is most beautiful when it flies. Great wings spread six or seven feet in width and neck tucked neatly between the shoulders, it skims two or three feet above the water, looking for all the world like a China Clipper on its way to Hawaii. Its voice is an inelegant squawk that in no wise matches the grace of the heron's appearance, but it is a tolerable disappointment in an otherwise splendid creature.

Equally splendid is the common egret, which strides along our dock with the aplomb if not quite the unquestioned authority of the heron. Although built along much the same lines, the egret is shorter, standing no more than three feet tall (I would estimate our heron to be no less than four feet in height from its feet to the top of its head). Its legs and beak are yellow, and its feathers a bright, impossible white that makes it shine brilliantly in the morning light. The egret is also more numerous than the great blue heron, and in the mornings of low tide, scores of them can be seen picking around in the mudflats of the bay, grubbing for worms and landlocked herring in the company of their shorter, stockier cousins, the snowy egrets, with their black legs, black beaks, and tufts of feathers jutting rakishly from the back of their heads.

My favorite bird is the brown pelican, although it is with us normally only during the fall and early winter months. In flocks of anywhere from ten to twenty birds, the pelicans swoop over our bay dramatically, their great beaks pointed at an angle toward the water. They are more cumbersome than the terns, yet remarkably agile when they spot the flash of something moving under the water. Often from a height of fifty or sixty feet, they will suddenly stop in their ponderous flight, fold their wings, and fall to the water with a splash like that of a dropped safe. When as many as twenty of them are feeding simultaneously close enough to the houseboat, the sound is like that of a waterfall. As large as they are, their flight is of a beauty to rival that of the gull's, and as sensitive; I have seen a pelican skim six inches above the water for a distance of at least one hundred yards, and never once move its wings.

There are more, so many more: the brown-flecked sandpipers and their little brothers, the sparrow-sized peeps, which gather in tightly-bunched flocks and fly across the water in a rythmic flap-and-glide sequence that shows flashes of their white bellies like the signal of a semaphor; the grebes, which spend most of their time under water, but rise long enough for you to note their tuxedo markings of black back and white front and the antic tuft of feathers that annotate the back of their heads; the white-beaked coots that can do no more toward flying than a frantic flapping and splashing across the water; the black-crested night herons, which huddle with thick necks and hunched shoulders like ghosts in the night, until the sun begins to cut through the mists of early morning; the mallards and wood ducks which paddle around in the spring with their little families strung out behind them; the cormorants, who gather by the hundreds and sit on the water for hours before one of them takes to the air with its long neck stretched out in front of him like an arrow, to be followed by another and another and another, until a single-file line of them reaches across the water's horizon into the haze of distance. . . .

Sitting at our kitchen table or on the front deck, we have studied the birds, and we have learned some things the field guides and ornithological books do not tell you. We have learned, for example, that gulls have developed a game, of sorts. There is a line of six old pilings in the water just off our deck. These are popular with the gulls for the puposes of idle perching. One day, all six of the pilings were occupied when a gull approached the first piling. It landed, dislodging the gull in possession, which then flapped over to the second piling and dislodged its occupant, which went over to the third piling. This continued down the line, until the last dislodged bird swooped all the way back up to the first piling, where the whole business began again. We have seen this happen many times since, and have concluded that the birds are simply entertaining themselves by engaging in the bird equivalent of musical chairs.

We have learned something even more puzzling—that the snowy egret, that lovely, delicate creature, has a mindless instinct for killing. At low tide, a small pool of water is left in front of our deck. It is frequently crowded with thousands of landlocked bay herring. At such times, we have seen one or two egrets simply lay waste to those helpless fish. Their necks pulled back in striking position like the body of a rattlesnake and their heads cocked with one eye on the water, the egrets begin killing the herring with a mechanical regularity, their beaks flashing into the water to spear them, shake them until dead, then toss the bodies onto the surface of the water. For hours this will go on, until the pool is a mass of dead fish. The birds do not eat them. They just kill them. We wonder if they are practicing their art, saving the fish for later consumption, or, as seems more likely, simply killing for the sheer joy of killing, as the mink and the ferret are said to do.

These are important things to know about, to wonder about, surely as important as the daily Dow-Jones averages or the supermarket inventory list or the latest craven scandal to ooze from the halls of government. It is the houseboat that has given us the opportunity to learn some things from a world that is no less real because it has nothing to do with the making of money or the exercise of power. Whenever someone asks me, as people are wont to do, why on earth I choose to live such a life, with all its drawbacks, I remember such things. I remember, too, the storms that have put me in touch with the realities of life and thus more closely in touch with myself. I remember the shared joys of privacy, warmth, and love that Joan and I have found here. I remember cold and foggy mornings when the whole world has seemed to have disappeared, leaving us wonderfully abandoned. I remember the sounds of the birds, the sight of the mountain ahead of us, the feel of a houseboat moving with the waves, the mute glory of a sunset in September coloring both sky and water. I tell people none of these things, but I remember them, and I bless myself for a lucky man.

Homeland North

A COAST MARKS THE BOUNDARY between what we know and what we can only guess, and is therefore a proper home for poets. This coast was home once for a very great poet, indeed. Sitting in his monk-like cell of a room at the top of Hawk Tower near Carmel, Robinson Jeffers knew many things. One of the things he knew best was the sea, for this thin, eaglefaced man could look down on it from his hand-built aerie of rock, could hear its faint thunder come rolling up the hill from the rocks below, smell its salt spray, guess at its eternality and at the beginnings of all of us. It was here he could write that:

> *I gazing at the boundaries of granite and spray, the established*
>   *sea-marks, felt behind me*
> *Mountain and plain, the immense breadth of the continent,*
>   *before me the mass and doubled stretch of water.*

It was here that he made the beautiful Tamar dance her lonely ritual of death, "while the sea moved on the bed of her eternity." And it was here that he put the poet's impromatur on what coastal peoples have always known in their hearts: "The tides are in our veins."

It is the function of poets to be historians of the spirit, to remind us who we have been, who we are, perhaps even who we might become. Certainly, Jeffers' sea-poetry does so for me. To read his muscular, awkward, profoundly forceful lines is like opening a book on myself, as if the poet were peeling away the layers of delusion, self-importance, and gaseous certitude to which blood and mind are heir, leaving me briefly, tantalizingly, with the shadowed hint of my essence. He touches me as no other poet ever has, and I think it is because I share, however imperfectly, something of the dimensions of love and awe he brought to his contemplation of the sea. He had a sense of forever, that man, as if he could put his hand on a great surf-ridden rock and feel the thrust of every wave against stone, feel the centuries wear it down to a spray of sand broadcast along a crescent of glistening beach. Sometimes, some very rare times, I think I may have sensed something close to that kind of infinitude.

Curiously, to me at least, it is not the homeland of my youth that comes into my mind's-eye when I read Jeffer's poetry, or even his own landscape of Carmel and Big Sur with its pines and rocks and pimordial mountains plunging thousands of feet straight into the sea. Rather, it is the North Coast I think about, for its crumbling headlands, its rocky coves, its wraiths of mist and fog, its dark medieval forests and heaving, punishing surf are elements only his stark, angular phrasing and sense of time could have captured. His poet's eye would have seen it as I see it, I think, and his skill would have given it voice. He might even have learned to love this North Coast as I have come to love it. For this harsh, unwelcoming shore, so unlike the soft, enfolding landscape of my youth, has become a kind of second homeland for me, calling out to something essential in the middle-aged man just as the South Coast called out to something in the boy. And in this new homeland there is a town, a tiny weathered clutch of buildings gathered outlandishly on a broken bluff above the sea. It is called Mendocino City, and it has become so much a part of what I feel for the North Coast that I cannot think of one without the other. Jeffers might have understood this.

My first season in Mendocino came in the winter of 1969, and it began without much promise. I needed a place removed from civilization in order to finish a book on the Colorado River. Mendocino came highly recommended by friends, and the idea of completing the book in such a place—160 miles north of San Francisco and about as far, emotionally or geographically, from the Colorado River you could expect to get on a limited budget—had a certain illogic that appealed to me. So early in February, I arranged to rent a house for two weeks, packed up some $2,000 worth of photographs and two years of research notes, and boarded the late afternoon bus for a town I hadn't seen.

Five hours later, after an interminable wait for a transfer in Santa Rosa, I arrived in Mendocino. It was dark and raining; pelting sheets of water obliterated the outlines of the town and smeared its few lights against a backdrop of oblivion. I stepped down from the bus—the only one of five passengers to do so—and walked with the driver around to the baggage compartment. He lifted the compartment's hatch: no baggage. Two thousand dollars worth of photographs, two years of research, books, papers, typewriter, clothes: not there.

"Whereinhell is my baggage?"

The driver looked uncomfortable. "Uh, well, it's not here."

I fumbled though my wallet and produced baggage checks. "It's got to be here," I croaked, thrusting the checks into his startled face.

"There's been some mistake," he pointed out, reaching into bureaucratic antiquity for the proper phrase. "Let me make a phone call."

He took my checks and stepped inside the Mendocino Hotel's office, which obviously doubled as the town's bus station. I stood outside under the sidewalk overhang and eyed the local tavern wistfully. It was closed. Ten minutes later, he emerged, looking triumphant.

"Well, I found your stuff. It was put on the wrong bus when you transferred in Santa Rosa."

"Where is it—Denver?"

"No, Lakeport."

Lakeport? I hadn't even heard of Lakeport, but the driver patiently explained that it was about a hundred miles south and east of Mendocino, near Clear Lake. He explained further that my AWOL baggage would have to be put on a bus for Santa Rosa in the morning, then transferred to the San Francisco bus, then transferred again in San Francisco that afternoon for arrival in Mendocino the following night. It sounded about as uncomplicated as three-dimensional chess to me, and I speculated aloud on the possibility of the stuff ending up in Marrekech. But there was nothing for it but to contract with local livery service and be transported to my home in the woods a mile outside the town, where I slept the sleep of the stricken.

Late the next morning, after combing my hair with a fork I'd found in the kitchen, I rambled into town through a dripping, gray-green rain forest and past scattered farm houses that sat hunched and weathered beneath a sky already lowering for another day's rain. A cow studied me with minor curiosity as I stood on the last rise of the road into town and looked down upon the place that was supposed to have provided me with serenity. Mendocino was a study in mist-ridden grays and whites hunkered under a black sky, a jumbled ramshackle town that spread over perhaps a square quarter mile, featuring aging water towers and the spire of a local church, which loomed in the haze like an arrow pointed at the heart of the devil. Beyond the town was the wind-driven sea, slamming itself against the steep, crumbling headlands of Mendocino Bay, and on a hill behind the town was a cemetery looking like something designed for a Bela Lugosi movie.

Shivering, I walked down into the town, past weed-grown feedlots, New England salt boxes with warped foundations, leaning fences, and occasional parked cars, which looked abandoned. The few people I saw on the streets walked rapidly, heads down and bodies bent against the increasingly damp wind. Even Main Street, a narrow, onesided thoroughfare that looked across an open pasture to the sea, was nearly deserted. I stepped into the hotel's coffee shop and had breakfast. By the time I had finished, the rain had started again, and there seemed little recourse but to step into Dick's Place two doors down the street; both the weather and the circumstances seemed to warrant a little hot brandy for the heart's ease.

Dick's Place, I discovered after several brandies, was a noble saloon, a spartan establishment that was a place of serious purpose, not cocktail lounge frivolity. The gloom of the day and my circumstances penetrated even here, however, so when the weather lifted momentarily I went outside again. The wind was caterwauling, but over it I could hear the sound of the sea. Inspired by the brandy and possibly following some primordial urge to gauge my problems against more eternal profundities, I made my way out to the edge of the point southwest of the town, where I stood like an abandoned Ishmael watching the gray crashing of the sea, while grisly images of a ruined career slithered through my mind.

A long rift developed in the clouds, revealing the sun and a patch of incredibly blue sky. To the left of the point and a hundred feet below me was a small cove whose beach was littered with driftwood. As I absent-mindedly watched the surf coming into the beach, there suddenly appeared from behind a pile of driftwood logs ten long-haired young people, boys and girls together, who skipped hand-in-hand into the waves and frolicked there in that Bering-like water until they could stand it no longer, then turned, and laughing at one another ran back behind the logs. They had been naked—absolute starkers. While my somewhat boggled mind was trying to assimilate what I had just seen, the sun lit upon Mendocino itself, sparkling against the windows of Main Street. From a distance of a quarter mile, the town looked for all the world like the combination of a New England fishing village and a movie-set cowboy town. I can't maintain that I had a vision at that moment, exactly; but it did occur to me then that if I could stop wallowing in self-pity long enough, I might discover that I had come to a rather remarkable place. I turned back to Main Street, a little warmer now in all respects.

And that evening, just as the bus driver had promised, my baggage arrived.

That was the beginning, and it was not without its unpleasant aspects. Yet over the next two weeks, when the job I had come north to do allowed me the time for investigation, I

found that my instincts had been right: Mendocino was a remarkable little town. It rained almost all the time I was there, but I managed to nose into most of the town's alleys and byways, became acquainted with several of its many cats, who ornamented the fences and rooftops when I walked in on rainless mornings, and talked to lumbermen, hippies, storekeepers, housewives, and artists. In short, I learned enough about Mendocino in two weeks to know that I would be coming back. I did come back, and have been coming back ever since, attempting to absorb the town and distill from it those qualities that had marked it in my memory as something unique.

The most apparent of those qualities is the town's architecture. In our accelerated society, where we are too busy building to build beautifully, there tends to be a deadly sameness to our architecture. Suburbias mimic one another and cities emulate Manhattan. Against this, Mendocino positively shouts individuality and charm. Like most of the towns along the North Coast, Mendocino was founded by transplanted New Englanders, and the spare, almost austere architecture of that region is well represented in the town—particularly by the first Presbyterian Church, since designated a State Historical Landmark. Most of the houses are old, and one—known locally as the Heeser House—goes back to the early 1850s. Many are well-preserved; others little better than crumbling shacks held together by hope and baling wire. The generally rustic air of the town is punctuated by still-functioning water towers, board sidewalks that creak beneath your feet, and some of the most wonderful fences you could imagine, from wrought iron to elaborately contrived picket. All of this has inspired cries of "picturesque" and "quaint," words that seem to me do the town little justice. This is a living town, after all, not some kind of picture postcard. Through accident, luck, and now determination, it has held out against the visissitudes of time so that you can wander through its back streets—occupied mainly by inquisitive dogs and kids on bicycles—and forget, for a while, that this is the latter end of the twentieth century. That's not picturesque or quaint. It's damned sensible.

Much of the determination to keep Mendocino a generally successful refugee from the twentieth century has come from its recent micro-boom as a center for artists impelled north by the beauty of a land wedded to the sea. And much of that boom, everyone is willing to admit, is the responsibility of William Zacha, who came north from the Bay Area more than ten years ago, opened an art gallery, then conceived and executed the Mendocino Art Center, a rambling collection of buildings on a rise at the northwestern edge of the town. When Zacha arrived, the town was comparatively moribund. A long dependence upon lumbering, the region's principle industry, ended when the town's last mill closed down in 1931, and there were only 500 people left. Today, there are 1,300, many of them supported by the Art Center and other facilities devoted to the manufacture and sales of arts and crafts. With an artist's eye, Zacha and some of his colleagues (painter Dorr Bothwell, for example) have refurbished many of the town's early buildings, retaining both their functionality and their charm, and have inspired others to do likewise. All this has resulted in a sense of style and a sense of scale.

Scale is notable in Mendocino. This is a people-sized town, with all the physical attributes common to Hollywood's interpretation of small-town America as it may or may not have existed. In Mendocino it exists. Not only is it possible to walk almost anywhere you would care to go, it is comprehensible on just about any other level. There is one small, but genuine hotel and one inn; there is one bank; there are two full-time restaurants and two which serve dinners only; there is no police station, no movie house (although the Art Center does show weekend films); there is one post office and one volunteer fire department; there are two service stations, two grocery stores, two taverns, two churches, and two graveyards. It is difficult to get confused in Mendocino, impossible to get lost. Time is slowed, urgency deteriorates, and life is expanded to include the smell of the sea-wind, the sound of a crowing rooster, the sight of a spavined white horse nibbling in a tiny pasture, the taste of flapjacks and coffee at the Sea Gull Inn.

Architecture, scale, and time arrested are three of the town's essential qualities. Yet other towns possess similar characteristics without coming close to achieving Mendocino's impact, at least in my experience. The answer must lie in the coast that provides the town with its setting, and there is something more here than the sheer beauty of it all. Mendocino's economic life was founded on the sea. Its nineteenth century mills fed lumber into the holds of steam schooners up from southern points, who used the town's bay as one of many "doghole" ports (big enough for a dog to crawl into, turn around, and crawl back out) scattered along the North Coast. A residue of that muscular heritage can be seen today in the disintegrating remains of the "dock" on the point southwest of the town. From there, loads of lumber, and occasionally passengers, were lowered by cable to little ships bobbing on heaving swells. But the relationship must go beyond this to a kind of spiritual level as well. On the North Coast, the ageless conflict between land and sea is apparent as it is nowhere else on the California coast. The edge of the land has been eaten away into unearthly formations, attesting to the power of that sea; the wind is constant and forcible; the persistent fogs as thick as gruel and as cold as a politician's heart. You cannot stand on that coast for an hour without feeling in your skin the pulse of all time and life. This is no place for the fainthearted. Those who live here have to be touched deeply by the knowledge that man and all his technology are susceptible to forces he just barely understands. That knowledge is woven deeply into the fabric of Mendocino's life. In balance with all else the place offers, it helps to explain why I stood near the edge of the sea that winter day in 1969 and knew that I had found a new homeland—and why I feel so today. For here is a rare and special place where a man may still feel a reaching out from the generations that have made him, and a kinship with the harsh and natural order of things.

As I write these words, I am sitting at the table of my Volkswagen camper—a serviceable beast for which I feel almost as much pained affection as I once felt for the family Yacht that carried me so often from home to homeland. The camper is parked on a bluff at Salt Point State Park some sixty miles below Mendocino. It is morning, and the sea moving in the cove below me is almost lost in the fog that is so much a part of this coast in the summer months that those who call the region home breathe it in without thinking about it, as residents of Los Angeles breathe in smog. The sea is very quiet. Even the gulls seem subdued, their cries muffled in rags of fog. Far out on the water, completely invisible, a fisherman's boat is spinning by, the sound of its outboard motor cutting into the heavy silence with an eerie whine. I am sitting here trying to write finish to a book, which is the hardest thing a writer has to do.

For no writer ever feels he has said all that he should have said about something so important to his life, as this shore of the sundown sea has been important to mine. There is another bookful of words left unwritten, perhaps never to be written, for most of those words are questions to which there will probably never be answers.

Yet if I must finish, let me end by questioning one of my own assumptions. I have called the memoried coast of my youth my landscape of freedom, and have implied at various times that the one thing this coast has given me more valuable than all the rest has been the sense of freedom. But am I dealing in illusions when I talk of freedom? No boy, no man, is free, no matter what his landscape. There is too much we simply cannot escape; we are caught up in the web of ourselves, trammeled and programmed to such a degree by genes, inclinations, and instincts that the decisions we think we make ourselves are made for us. It is the Hindus who define freedom as a prison in which we are equidistant from all walls, and the balance which that definition suggests is probably all that we can hope of freedom. When I walk a stretch of coast, I do not, like Thoreau heading west, "walk free," not truly.

Yet there is a value in the very illusion of freedom which this coast has given me, for it has kept me from becoming that dull and joyless thing: the man who questions nothing, who accepts his limitations, who is in fact devoid of illusion. Like the man in the *New Yorker* cartoon who proclaims his Americanism by declaring there is nothing he will not tolerate, the man without illusion is without hope, for that is what illusion is. And the man without hope will die knowing nothing, nothing at all.

If I cannot have freedom, then, I can at least have its illusions, given to me by the landscape of sun, sea, and wind. With luck and a measure of dreams I may die with some of those illusions intact, with some of that hope left to carry me into the mysteries that will be waiting on the other side.

This book is done. Joan is waiting for me on the houseboat. I will want to see my children. It is time to break camp and leave these broken, wind-battered slopes of the North Coast for the softer, less demanding world of work and daily living, where I find a measure of myself in those who love me, and even in some of those who do not. I will be back. I will always be back. But even as I prepare to leave, an image comes to me of a short, brown, solidly-built boy who is running on the shores of my memory. The sun is low in the sky and bounces off the water with a painful light, silhouetting him. I can see him and I wish that I could reach out to touch him, speak to him out of our shared past. *Selah*, I would say to him. Blessings, small boy. Do not forget this.

This book was printed at
Phelps/Schaefer Litho-graphics Co., San
Francisco in November 1973. The type face is
Palatino, set by Holmes Composition Service, San Jose.
The dust jacket stock is Strathmore Chroma Text,
the end-papers are Multicolor, and the basic
stock is Beckett Text. The cover cloth is
Columbia Mills Bolton Buckram natural finish.
The book was bound by Filmer Brothers, San Francisco.

Design by John Beyer.